CW01161008

Long Stays in GERMANY

A COMPLETE, PRACTICAL GUIDE TO LIVING AND WORKING IN GERMANY

J.A.S. ABECASIS-PHILLIPS

DAVID & CHARLES
Newton Abbot   London

HIPPOCRENE BOOKS
New York

For the late Edna Lady Joseph

British Library Cataloguing in Publication Data

Abecasis-Phillips, John A. S.
   Long stays in Germany.
   1. West Germany – Visitors' guides
   I. Title
   914.3'04878

   ISBN 0–7153–9420–7

© John A. S. Abecasis-Phillips 1990

All rights reserved. No part of this
publication may be reproduced, stored
in a retrieval system, or transmitted,
in any form or by any means, electronic,
mechanical, photocopying, recording or
otherwise, without the prior permission
of David & Charles Publishers plc

Printed in Great Britain
by Billings & Sons   Worcester
for David & Charles Publishers plc
Brunel House   Newton Abbot   Devon

Published in the United States of America
by Hippocrene Books Inc
171 Madison Avenue, New York, NY 10016
ISBN 0-87052-595-6 (United States of America)

Contents

	Preface	4
	Introduction	5
1	Preparations	12
2	Money	17
3	The Social Net	26
4	Education	35
5	Transport	41
6	The Move and Accommodation	49
7	Being Moneywise	62
8	Business Relationships	71
9	Closer Relationships	84
10	The Language	109
11	Communication with Home: The Postal System	114
12	Bureaucracy	120
13	Law: Under Constant Supervision	127
14	Tips for Students	131
15	Understanding Current Events	147
16	German Culture	163
17	Relaxation	173
18	Staying On?	183
	Epilogue: Looking over the Wall	191
	Acknowledgements	195
	Bibliography	197
	Index	198

Preface

Originally I was a short stayer and then became a long stayer in Germany. I have written for the short stayer in the past, now I offer this for the long stayer moving to, settling down and in, ultimately possibly staying on in West Germany. Germany is unique, *especially* for English-speaking visitors of British or Celtic stock. My aim has been to explain the uniqueness so that you can truly feel at home there among the old and the new as expressed in the two motifs on the front cover. I hope I succeed and that your long stay in Germany will be all the more worthwhile as a result.

Introduction

Germany is the richest country in the European Community. As is so often said: Germany may have lost the war, but most certainly won the peace. The wealth involved is however not just material; local cultural riches are immense. Moving to Germany means changing to a different way of life. True, most Germans speak some English, which removes some of the foreignism from moving to their country. Yet there is much that is different and this book aims to make it less so.

A guide to a foreign country should be someone who is familiar with the local scene and can explain it. Having spent more than twenty years in Western Germany I feel able to explain the scene from the foreigner's point of view, especially the process of initiation and establishing a niche, whilst keeping the lines open to home. Living in Germany as a foreigner makes one very aware of being European or multi-national. It changes one's outlook on life and increases awareness of the advantages and disadvantages of living at home and/or abroad. Europeans who live in Germany need not give up all or even most contacts with home. Even for Americans this is true, especially for those serving in the forces. Air travel and improved communications have shrunk the world, extended horizons and improved a person's ability to master living in more than one country.

Moving to Germany means making a home there and this book is structured accordingly: preparations (including getting there), settling in, settling down, and finally deciding whether or not to stay on. All these stages involve becoming acquainted with the country and the different way of life that is in some respects so different from home. The whole relationship between State and citizen, work ethic and attitude to life (scale of priorities and inherent tensions) creates a different framework for living. The world wars, the conditions that produced them, revolution, Nazi terror, national bankruptcy and subsequent monetary reforms, the split between East and West are influences that create an

Introduction

attitude to life based on realism and caution, in many respects the opposite of the traditionally relaxed, relatively easy English way of life.

The tourist's view of Germany seen on posters featuring dream-King Ludwig's castles, fairytale Black Forest or Bavarian mountain villages is one kind of reality. Behind the façade is a completely different way of life, not Third Man stuff but the nitty-gritty of making a living, dealing with bureaucracy, renting or buying a house, educating the children, buying a car, going on holiday, arranging accident and health insurance, saving for retirement, and so on. All this is set against a vigorous cultural life from the classics to pop, tremendous energy and dedication that offer great opportunities for integration on the part of the long stayer. The complication for the foreign visitor is of course that this all takes place in a foreign language requiring considerable effort on his or her part to become involved. But it is manageable. You just have to be patient.

At the practical level, the great thing in Germany is that things work; you can turn on a hot water tap and out comes hot water, you turn on a radiator and the room is soon warm; trains and buses normally arrive on time; there are almost no strikes, and goods are of reasonable quality. Life is very comfortable. The standard of living is generally high. At the spiritual level, the younger generation did not experience the last war; the older generation recognises that modern Germany has changed since Hitler's day.

Whatever the reasons, the idea of moving to Germany is more appealing than ever today. This book deals with the practicalities: housing, education, bureaucracy — the whole business of preparing the move, of settling in and down in a foreign country which, if found acceptable, might become home.

Considerable personal and family psychology is involved before even considering a long stay in Germany. And it is here that the glossy brochures are so misleading. In *Coping with Germany* (see reading list), aimed at the short term visitor, the author attempted to get behind the sausage-eating, beer-swilling tourist attitude to visiting Western Germany. Here, we go into greater detail.

Background information will help you to understand the German way of doing things, which may well be different from home. Germany, perhaps more than other countries, because of its recent history, requires more understanding. However descriptions alone cannot always provide a short cut to unravelling German imponderables. It is part of accepting that one is a visitor, in fact a foreigner in another country with different traditions and a different way of life. Settling in involves trying to understand what is going on and assimilating new ways of doing things before the next stage of settling down arrives. Some people feel challenged to insist on doing things the British way and fail. The key is to accept a different way of life. It is not always easy.

The key to understanding Germany lies in what Germans say of their own country: it is a *Beamtenstaat* (a state of officials) together with an understanding that German democracy is very new; and furthermore that, as Germans also admit, they tend to go in for extremes, do things very thoroughly indeed, which takes some getting used to for the visitor.

Cultural and social flexibility are essential for a long stay. For a short stay it is different. During a long stay, home, be it America or England, recedes necessarily into the background. Hankering after it will prejudice settling down. One must make the break, however temporary. The better informed one is about Germany beforehand, the less disturbing the cultural shock will be.

Possibly some aspects of German life, which will be explained here, may seem strange to the English-speaking reader, especially descriptions of the German attitude to bureaucracy. You may think that too much space is given to the subject. However most people find that it is not easy to understand all the regulations that must be observed on arrival in Germany and whilst settling in. This book aims to help you master such regulations.

It helps to look around your own home first, think of the friends you will miss seeing, and those things that have become so much a part of your life that it would be difficult to imagine having to do without. You should not over-dramatise their importance or underestimate the feeling of loss. For example, it is difficult to get a decent, strong cup of tea in Germany or to buy Marmite; English newspapers are expensive, cable television (ie Sky Channel) is not yet nationwide. If these things do not matter, fine, but obviously some aspects of home life associated

Introduction

with England are difficult to do without. English education for your children is just one example and this will be considered in greater detail later. The subject of pension rights is another.

The above is not intended to frighten you off contemplating a long stay in Germany. Quite the contrary, but it is essential to try and establish beforehand whether or not you and your family are ready for a long stay in Germany. You must decide this for yourself. The aim of this book is to make the decision easier, although ultimately only experience will tell whether you chose wisely.

Like any other country, Germany is changing all the time, possibly more so than other countries because of its inner dynamism and because, situated where it is, government and people are sensitive to the international political climate. You are not moving to a country in a political vacuum. Nothing is as settled and secure as it is at home. There is order but no certainty about things. You must live with Russian troops sometimes barely 50km (30 miles) away. Of course after a time, like the Germans, you do forget them, but a different situation is involved and it should be recognised. Indeed, recent changes in Eastern Germany have made this book more topical than ever – and increased the difficulties of keeping the contents up to date.

This book, which has grown out of the experience of twenty five years of living in Germany, tries also to give the flavour of Germany. What is the German flavour? Is there such a thing? And if there is, will you taste it? The answer becomes clear when you compare the experiences which you have here in Germany with those back home, at the pub, at the post office, in the train, at university, in shops, etc. Personal relationships are more difficult to compare in this way. Is it the different institutions or the people? Do the institutions affect the people or merely reflect them; or both?

Institutions reflect history, and history has tended to make Germany into an *Ordnungsstaat* (a well regulated state) where people unquestioningly tend to do what they are told. In the Peasant Revolt of 1525 many peasant leaders were killed, and the March Revolution of 1848, a middle class revolution, was followed by the Restoration; while Bismarck introduced a *Sozialstaat* (universal insurance for workers and so on), this was a revolution from above and not from below. His style of

Introduction

government was more authoritarian than democratic; and it continued until the revolution in 1918 that ended the monarchy, and introduced the Weimar Republic which did not last very long and by default led to the Nazi takeover under Hitler, war and chaos. Western democracy, as such, was first introduced to Germany by the Allies and is thus a relatively late grafting of free institutions on a formerly enslaved people. Moreover, the other part of Germany was still under communist dictatorship or oligarchy until recently. The citizens of the so-called German Democratic Republic have only just begun to enjoy the taste of democracy and freedom. True, in Western Germany, there were the student protests of the 1960s, the violent protest movements of the environmentalists, the formation of the Green Party and other signs that Germans are no longer just a nation of obedient, law-abiding citizens who will always obey the State no matter what. So there has been a change of attitude.

Most Germans are fairly law abiding and as a foreigner from an English-speaking country, living in Germany, you will no doubt soon become aware that you are in a country where most things are laid down in writing and where there seem to be laws to regulate every aspect of human life. You may feel that everything is a trifle too well ordered and organised. Doubtless you will get used to it, indeed begin to appreciate the advantages — and there are advantages — of living in such a well ordered society. At other times you may become suffocated and frustrated by it. Patience is a virtue, and an ability to understand the German way of life from a historical perspective will undoubtedly help. You may feel sometimes that too much freedom is enjoyed to the detriment of those who use it. University students sometimes appear to me to abuse the academic freedom they possess to the detriment of their own studies. This is a highly subjective opinion, but it is tempered by the view that in some areas of university life students accept too much control where they would, in fact, be better off in rejecting it.

A posting for those on government service:
This book is addressed not only to those who have a choice of whether or not to move to Germany, but also to those whose choice is limited. They may be in the armed services, with the

Introduction

British Council or America House, or in the diplomatic corps or other government service and have little or no option but to move with their families to Germany. Moving with your eyes open is obviously better than moving with them shut, with yourself and your family totally unprepared, save for an official briefing with the assurance that married quarters are provided and that someone local will answer your questions. According to the briefing, you need merely to arrange for the removals' company to come. The question of education does not arise because generous allowances finance continued attendance at independent schools. So what are you worrying about? It's just another posting.

So why do you need this book? Quite simply, to make the most of the opportunities offered. I followed my stepfather, who was a soldier, to Egypt and West Germany without getting much out of it because I was sealed off from the locals for my own safety in Egypt and, in accordance with the no-fraternisation regulations after the war, in Germany. Nowadays people are cut off simply by the language, but this need not be; a little encouragement and information might help at the beginning to make the process of living in Germany more comprehensible and thus worthwhile and enjoyable.

German attitude to foreigners

English-speaking foreigners usually belong to the middle or upper income brackets as opposed to the so-called *Gastarbeiter* (immigrant workers) from Turkey, Italy and Spain who usually do manual work. The problems of the immigrant workers are more basic than those that concern English-speaking long stayers and the German attitude to foreigners varies accordingly.

The larger cities are cosmopolitan; foreigners constitute more than 20 per cent of the population in some cities. Germans are definitely not isolationists. They are interested in foreign affairs and media coverage is comprehensive. The average German is interested in foreign visitors and is willing, indeed eager, to learn about their way of life. Many Germans are touchingly dedicated in their efforts to learn both English and about English-speaking countries.

Introduction

The sequence of chapters
While I have tried to accord each main subject its own chapter, it has not always been possible to provide the right sequence for every reader. Parents wondering whether or not to educate their children at home or in Germany need to take the decision *before* moving to Germany and this is only one of the preparatory decisions they need to take. A student deciding on whether or not to attend a German university will not be so concerned with the preparatory decisions his or her parent might take involving the whole family. I have therefore put education near the beginning and 'Tips for students' near the end.

I have not separated the chapter on transport specifically into before and after the move but let the decision about taking you car with you to Germany merge with the purchase of one when you arrive. Where relevant, I have aimed at a natural progression from before the move to arrival in Germany in each chapter. Where helpful, I have given cross-references in the text, so that you can adjust the sequence of information to your own liking. In places I have gone into great detail on relatively minor matters, such as the postal services, in order to clarify a more important point on a higher level (in this case German bureaucracy). You can skip the boring details but in doing so you might miss the general picture of the German way of life that emerges. Everyday things can take up so much time if not mastered, and because they can take up so much time they are indicative of the uniqueness of the German way of and attitude to life, especially for the visitor of British or Celtic origin. I want you to understand what is going on so that you can come to terms with it and settle in more quickly and really enjoy life in the country.

1
Preparations

Employment — getting a job — securing employment — be sure of getting your job first
Undoubtedly it is better to be assured of employment before going to Germany rather than looking for something on the spot after giving up a job at home. Some young people do do this and are either bitterly disappointed with what they get, or have to make do with odd jobs to survive. Some find nothing at all and return home penniless or with their funds drastically reduced. Much frustration could have been avoided with a little foresight.

First of all unless you want to work as a labourer (and here there is considerable competition from Italians, Greek and Turkish unskilled labour), there is little point in looking for skilled work without the necessary qualifications. Germans demand paper qualifications and take degrees, diplomas, certificates, references and the like very seriously. They are most exacting and professional in this respect; they have little respect for the so-called gifted amateur or, to put it another way, even if you can do the job in question, but haven't the necessary paper qualification, then forget it. Having got the job, the piece of paper is still essential. Formalities are taken most seriously especially now, with high local unemployment. There remains the possibility that if no-one else is available and someone is needed to do a particular job, then the rules will be bent — a teacher who is desperately needed but who does not possess the best qualifications will be taken on but even in teaching there is high unemployment. It can be worthwhile, however, enquiring on the spot, perhaps during a holiday. It pays to get to know people personally, just to absorb something of the atmosphere of a place and to judge the local employment situation. But do not burn your boats before leaving the UK or the States and thus be forced to beg for work. The balmy days of the sixties are over when jobs could be easily obtained.

Preparations

German job prospects — how does one go about it? — importance of the right attitude

This book cannot provide a comprehensive guide to employment in Germany and it would be dishonest to suggest that in a few pages much real help can be given in this respect. However, it is possible to give some pointers in the right direction. They relate to what has already been said in the introduction about the desire to move to a foreign country and give up one's own country. They also relate to settling in and settling down. First, the psychological attitude has to be right. Second it helps if your own work ethic is in tune with the prevailing German version. This is not to suggest that all Germans are industrious, but it is to state that the German attitude to work is serious. Work is accorded a higher social status than, for example, in the United Kingdom; it is possibly also higher than in the States. Again this is not to assert that Germans are all work and no play. Quite the reverse is true, but certain demands are made on employees that some British people might initially find hard to accept. The unions (and this will be discussed later) play a different role from their counterparts in the UK and the States. Although work is taken seriously, the tangible rewards in terms of a high standard of living are great, but so is the effort necessary to achieve it. A special element of stress is involved which is peculiar to their structure and the way that things are done. It is difficult to generalise, nonetheless the informality of business and working life which exists in English-speaking countries, is lacking in Germany. For someone thinking of working in Germany it might be well to accept at this stage that there is usually a sharp division between work and play; or, simply, between being on the job and at home. It is possible to work at a German university for fifteen years and still not address colleagues by their Christian names or have even been invited to their homes.

However, no judgements should be made until the reasons for such a different work framework have been considered. The potential long stayer, as opposed to the short term visitor, needs to understand the background to such social differences before he can truly judge for himself.

Not all of this different working atmosphere is necessarily strange or difficult to adjust to. Indeed, certain aspects may be considered to be a welcome improvement on home. It depends

Preparations

on the person concerned. At this stage it is essential to realise that some adjustment in workstyle might have to be made as in lifestyle too, because the reward of both is a higher standard of living. It can be summed up by saying that German work procedures, which are by no means perfect, nonetheless produce the goods, although the economy is coming under strain from increased competition from abroad. However most long stayers in work are better off than many British and a significant percentage of American colleagues.

Employment situation in Germany
When looking for a job in Germany do not forget that there is considerable unemployment (over 7.6 per cent in November 1989) in the Federal Republic and that therefore one is lucky to find employment. But there is still a shortage, as in every country, of qualified staff. Unemployment tends to be regional, relative to the fall in demand for coal and, formerly, steel (now recovering through rationalisation). An appreciating mark and falling dollar have made German exports more expensive and thus have led to a consequent fall in demand. The German economy is in the middle of an agonising restructuring process and demand for labour is falling. Strenuous efforts are being made to retrain people in high-tech, but the expense to the State is enormous at a time when there is a structural crisis in the government pension and State supervised health schemes. Germany is still a very prosperous country, but prosperity has its price, both social and economic. Finding work therefore may prove to be difficult, even impossible.

Having the right skills
Assuming you are fully qualified in your own profession and are considering moving abroad to Germany, the question is whether or not your qualifications at home are recognised in Germany, be it in a company (large or small), a school, university or other institution. Purely local American or British qualifications, which enable one to do a job at home, are not necessarily relevant for the equivalent German post, not only because of the different language but simply for the different way of working. German accountants and their British colleagues have differently structured work. Only in a wider Anglo-German context

Preparations

would their skills be mutually recognised and applicable. There are differences between English, American and German tax laws. British and American doctors and medical specialists, scientists, scholars and businessmen, assuming they could cope with the language, would be interchangeable with their German colleagues.

In any case, considerable interchange at different work levels goes on already, but there are obviously some borderline cases. The main question to resolve is whether or not you feel that you can in the long run be as effective at your job in Germany as back home. And it is this that you should take into consideration when looking for a job in Germany. The job description is therefore very important. Daily papers and specialist journals carry appointments columns, and a subscription to the weekend edition of the main German papers such as the *Frankfurter Allegemeine*, the *Süddeutsche* or *Die Zeit* might provide a useful supplement to such research.

Enquiries at the London offices of the larger German companies would obviously help further, even if just to confirm the name and address of the personnel manager in Germany. Specialist international employment agencies (see list of useful addresses at the back of the book) are also the obvious places to make further enquiries. It is difficult to lay down general rules to which there are obviously so many exceptions.

Employment prospects

1992, being almost upon us, has heralded mass take-overs of German and even American companies in Germany by British companies, for example, of the German *Wiener Wald* restaurants and *Burger King* by Grand Metropolitan. One imagines that this would provide extra opportunities for employment there; conversely German conglomerates seeking to take over British concerns, for example the Siemens/GEC attempted takeover of Plessey, would be seeking additional British staff.

There are no restrictions for citizens of the European Community, and thus of the United Kingdom, seeking employment, but there are restrictions for Americans and for nationals of other countries outside the Common Market.

In my experience it is not just the job itself but the people with whom one works who are important. Of course this holds for any

Preparations

post, but it is particularly difficult to gauge this in a foreign country and in a foreign language. Hence the importance of making good use of the interview, not only for probing by the potential employer, but to do some probing yourself. It is surprising how many people immediately rush back home after the interview, rather than staying on for just one more day to really have a look round. The flight is expensive but, if that is paid for by the firm, the extra cost of staying on a little to look around is probably minimal, and is presumably tax deductible.

'Take your time!' is an obvious piece of advice. Nothing is to be gained by hurrying. Moreover, learn to look with the eyes of the family as well, at the schools, the shops, the surroundings and, of course, at the housing.

Interview techniques

It is difficult to have an interview with a German executive or official where he or she will not be disturbed by the telephone or by a colleague simply opening the door, coming in and asking a question. You must have nerves of steel to concentrate like mad, hoping that the interviewer can do the same. It is a different way of doing things. You just have to get used to it. In time, of course, you will find yourself behaving in the same way. One of the first interruptions likely to occur is a welcome one; a secretary will ask whether you would like a cup of coffee. Say yes, because then your host can enjoy one too. It's in general a hurried, yet informal, way of doing business.

Young people looking for a job — internships and student exchanges

One way of finding out about the country, its people and the likely conditions of possible future employment is to make the most of student-exchange programmes whilst at university. Some student-exchange programmes include internships in Germany. Those who can choose their eventual employer would be wise to select the same type of company. Indeed the existence of such programmes — see chapter 14, *Tips for students* — might be a consideration in choosing a British or American university in the first place, given that from 1992 young people in the United Kingdom will have to think internationally.

2
Money

Assuming that you have a job, now for the main practicality: money. Money makes the world go round at home and especially abroad. Purely financial considerations might well have sparked off interest in moving to Germany in the first place. Let us examine the structure of German salaries. First it depends whether you are employed by the State and enjoy *Beamter* – official – status or are a salaried employee *(Angestellter)* employed by the State or a private company.

Salaries

If you are an *Angestellter*, your salary and allowances will probably be determined by a collective agreement signed by your employer or the group or confederation of employers to which he or she belongs, and one of the large trade unions like the *Deutsche Angestellten Gewerkschaft* (German Workers' Union). By examining a salary slip we can see how the system works.

First, in Germany wages and salaries are seldom paid in cash but usually into employees' bank or savings' bank accounts. Those working for the State usually receive their salaries at the beginning of the second week of the month. Other employers pay their workers at the end of the month. Salary or pay slips vary but many look like the one overleaf.

For State employees *(Beamten* and *Angestellten)* there is an official age *(Dienstalter)* based on the number of years you have been employed by the State, as opposed to your physical age *(Lebensalter)*, and payment is according to the former age.

Above, going from left to right, is the payment group *(Vergütungsgruppe)*, the salary group.

From this will be seen that the components of a wage or salary consist or can consist of:

Grundgehalt — basic wage or salary

Ortszuschlag — local allowance, paid dependent upon place of work where one is employed

Money

BEZIRKSFINANZDIREKTION ANSBACH
BEZUEGESTELLE BAYREUTH

Munchen,   22 b

4211	30029435
Arb Gr	Personalnummer

Mitteilung über Ihre Vergütung / Ihren Lohn
Blatt 1   Gültig ab   JANUAR 1989
Erläuterungen (Änderungsgründe):

Bitte bei allen Zuschriften angeben!

BFD ANSBACH BEZUEGESTELLE BAYREUTH
POSTFACH 11 03 53, 8580 BAYREUTH

Salary Group	Official Age	Temporary work: no of hours weakly	Married/Single	Spouse	Tax class	Children's allowance	Children	Religion	Insurance Group Contribution %	Health Insurance	Social Insurance	Unemployment Insurance
BAT2A	45	NEIN	VERH	.	I	.	.	VD	ZUSCH.	JA (2)	JA (1)	
										18,70	4,30	

Dienstalter	Sachbezüge o sonst Leistungen	Freibetrag lt. Lohnsteuerkarte	steuerpfl Bezug lfd Monat				
03.03.75			571709		610000	610000	
					583402	583402	

Von der Arbeitgeberleistung zur Zusatzversorgung sind im lfd Monat   Entgelt lfd Monat Zusatzversorgung
11693   571709

Aufgliederung des Bezuges	Lfd Monat DM Pf	Einm./Nach- oder Überzahlung DM Pf	Abzüge und Zusammenstellung	Lfd Monat DM Pf	Einm./Nach- oder Überzahlung DM Pf
GRUNDVERGUETUNG	469444		LOHNSTEUER TAB.A	160680	
ORTSZUSCHLAG	92265		RENTENVERS.	54548	
STELLENZUL.(232)	10000		ARBEITSLOSENVERS	12543	
SUMME	571709		SUMME	227771	

ZUSAMMENSTELLUNG

BRUTTOBETRAEGE	571709	000
KV-ZUSCHUSS	28800	
SUMME	600509	
SUMME ABZUEGE	227771	000
NETTO	372738	000

Überweisungsbetrag   3 727,38

Konto-Nr.: 1260220604
BLZ: 78020429

Vermerke

Money

Stellenzulage — extra payments eg, for overtime, holding examinations etc; coded numbers are given and list of such numbers is explained on the reverse. All this is on the left-hand side. On the right hand are the deductions (*Abzüge*) (debited on the pay-as-you-earn system) for health insurance (*Krankenkasse*), accident insurance, pension premiums and for unemployment benefit, etc.

Net earnings

The basic aim is usually clear; to make more money in relation to the local standard of living and to achieve an improved lifestyle. More money with a more expensive cost of living is not going to bring much improvement, but may achieve exactly the opposite. It is the relationships which are important, in particular rates of inflation, future prospects and especially net rather than gross earnings. If you are a businessman you will not need much coaching in this.

The deductions (*Abzüge*) usually amount to a third of your gross (*Brutto*) wage or salary, leaving the net (*Netto*) amount credited to your wage/salary account (*Girokonto*) held with the bank — see Banks. State employees receive a separate pay slip by post before the salary is transferred. This should be kept for tax purposes. You will receive the tax card (*Steuerkarte*) at the beginning of the year from the local authorities for handing to your employer, who will then return it at the end of the year stating how much income tax you have paid. Do not lose this form because it is time-consuming to get a replacement. The good thing about German salaries is that you are often paid a 13th month in November, conditional on having been employed for the full 12 months previously. Trade unions usually send their members a booklet giving the different salary scales.

The tax problem

This can be fiendishly complicated. Professional advice is well worth taking *before* moving to Germany and before returning to the UK from a long stay in Germany. Remember that *unless*, say as a teacher, you achieve local (German) tax exemption, under the terms of the relevant Double (ie, Anglo-German or American) Taxation Agreement, even if you obtain exemption

Money

from those countries' tax, you are still liable for German tax, which will be considered later. Being exempt from UK tax does not mean total exemption from tax.

Investment income

Obviously you will need to consult either your bank or broker on any changes necessary in your portfolio to make the most of any tax concessions relating to your future non-resident status for tax purposes. This is a highly technical matter for which it is well worth taking specialist advice, especially about private funds in England, which attract tax even after emigration as described above. You can be out of the country and resident abroad but still be classified as a UK resident (domiciled) for tax purposes. Even if you are entitled to a tax rebate because you have emigrated abroad, accountants' fees eat it up and it usually takes so long before it is repaid by the Inland Revenue, for which no interest is paid in compensation, that you sometimes begin to doubt the usefulness of the Double Taxation Treaty for the taxpayer as opposed to the revenue departments involved.

UK tax on overseas earnings in Germany

Total exemption from UK taxation on overseas earnings is usually only possible where the employment is full time and continuous with all attendant duties performed outside the UK, for at least one complete tax year ending 5 April *or* where the period is for 365 days or more, yet the complete tax year does not end on 5 April, that is until the end of the tax year itself. Where confusion may arise is in deciding whether the UK tax exemption status is affected by visits home. If you are absent for a complete tax year, exemption would only be forfeited if you visited the UK for one quarter of the total number of days from departure to the following 5 April; or if more than 91 days were spent in the UK in the first complete tax year, or more than 91 days on an average each year for any four consecutive tax years, or over the entire period of German residence if less than for four years.

Exemption would also be lifted if more than 182 days were spent in any one tax year or the long stayer intended to resume residence in Britain. Should the period of absence of the taxpayer amount to 365 days or more, yet not amount to one complete tax

Money

year ending 5 April, tax exemption is granted when the job for that period is performed in Germany.

The important thing to remember is that earnings in Germany are not exempt from British tax because they originate abroad, even if they are not remitted home. It depends upon the length of time you spend in Germany. To be exempt from UK tax, non-residence for tax purposes must be obtained; this status can be threatened by visits home of such duration that make the status questionable. Periods of residence in Germany may not be interrupted by visits home of more than 62 consecutive days. Tax-free status can also be prejudiced by repeated visits home, even if they total less than a sixth of the total time spent in Germany in any one tax year, which is the limit you are allowed to return home for without losing exemption.

The best thing is to ensure that throughout the time spent in Germany, visits do not exceed one-sixth of the total period from the date of original departure to the day before the date of the *next* proposed visit home. Otherwise German earnings are taxable in UK. However, percentage deductions may be claimable before assessment.

Tax: the calendar year

The essential difference when filing a German tax return is to remember that the German tax year is a calendar year, not as in UK from 4 April (of one year) to 5 April of the next year, but from 1 January to 31 December of the same year. This difference can cause chaos for UK citizens with investment income in Britain, which must be entered on the German tax return to claim the relevant tax allowance. The British tax year does not fit the German. The solution is to persuade the German inland revenue to accept the British tax year for purposes of UK investment income.

Double taxation agreements

Your tax position with regard to UK investment income will be determined by the Anglo-German Taxation Agreement. It is only sensible to obtain a copy of the agreement in English with the latest amendments. You may well find when you settle down in Germany that your accountant back home knows nothing about German tax law and your German account little about

21

Money

British tax legislation. I found it helpful to visit the Board of Inland Revenue Library at Somerset House and with permission read through the relevant papers myself. Do not leave things *entirely* to the experts. Or put it another way: an informed client gets better service.

How the Anglo-German Double Taxation Agreement system works is as follows. Assuming UK tax at a basic rate of 25 per cent, the UK inland revenue after due application return 50 per cent of UK tax paid ie 12½ per cent. The remaining 50 per cent of tax paid, ie 12½ per cent is then allowed against the German tax debt.

>   *Stage I* UK Investment Income for John Smith
>   Share Income £1,000 — 25% = £250
>   50% of that, ie 12½% returned 250 ÷ 2 = £125 —
>   can be claimed as a rebate
>
>   *Stage II* German taxable income
>   DM 60.000 — from which £125 x 3.20 = DM 400 —
>   may be deducted from German tax debt.

Preparing the documents

The problem of both the British and German inland revenue departments requiring the same documents (tax receipts) more or less simultaneously is that the British seem to take ages to process the application for rebate (possibly due to requiring additional clarification for sources of income, especially when this comes from trusts) which then delays submitting the local German tax return. Thus the British 5 April 1988 – 4 April 1989 tax rebate cannot be submitted until 6 April 1989, whereas the German tax return for the year 1 January – 31 December 1988 is due in by 1 May 1989, if you do not have an accountant (*Steuerberater*) or by 30 September 1989, if you do. As there is usually a delay of some months on the part of HM Inland Revenue for Foreign Dividends in dealing with applications for rebate and thus in returning tax receipts to the taxpayer, this holds up filing the German tax return. I had this problem for several years running and it usually meant applying for an extension in Germany entailing additional accountancy fees and frustration. Ultimately the local German inland revenue department agreed to accept a copy of the list of dividends

Money

and tax payable compiled by the UK accountant as proof of UK tax paid.

However, the German revenue department is by no means obliged to do this and is entitled to insist on seeing each individual tax receipt. To have all UK tax receipts issued with a second copy or photocopy and then have the copies duly authenticated is costly both in money and time. Moreover, there are always one or two that get mislaid. The solution is therefore for your UK accountant to let you have a copy of the list of stocks and shares he submits to the British inland revenue for a rebate, for filing with your German tax return.

Local taxes: exemption for teachers

As the Germans would say, taxes are a science *(Wissenschaft)* apart. Every general statement is subject to qualification. But there is good news, at least at the beginning, for groups such as teachers, who are granted local tax exemption for two years. Thereafter they pay German taxes. The respective Double Taxation Treaties between England and Germany and between Germany and the United States lay down the requirements.

Filing a local tax return

Going abroad can make your life more complicated and tax is an example of this. Though the German tax system is more complicated than the British, the latter recognises more tax deductions than the former, though the time spent in filing a tax return is considerable. One certainly earns the rebates. However the golden rule is file your return punctually, that is by the end of May, if you have no accountant, and by the end of September, if you do. Miss these deadlines and any subsequent extensions that may have been granted, and the Inland Revenue office *(Finanzamt)* will make an assessment that will exclude tax deductions. Ignore that assessment and you will be dunned.

Basically there are three or four returns to complete: income; wages or salary as an employee *(Einkommensteuer aus nicht selbstständiger Tätigkeit)*; income from other sources — such as freelance writing, etc *(Einkommen aus selbstständiger Tätigkeit)*; investment income: stocks and shares *(Einkommen aus Kapitalvermögen)*; capital (stocks and shares) and property on the value of which a wealth tax of 0.5% is levied regardless of

23

whether the fortune is held inland or abroad (*Kapitalvermögen*).

The main thing about German taxes is that considerable tax deductions are allowed in the form of expenses (*Betriebskosten*). The art of reducing one's tax debt is to keep account of all justifiable expenses, which means keeping all the relevant receipts.

For employees, journeys to work are accepted as an expense, but only one way, the journey there but not the return. It is simply calculated as a sum per kilometre, to date 42 Pfg (*Kilometre-Pauschalbetrag*) which is not just for petrol but for repairs and maintenance. Hence garage bills may not be claimed as an additional expense. Depending upon whether the business journey (*Dienstfahrt*) is within the country or abroad, an average daily allowance (*Tagespauschalsatz*) is allowed. It is possible to set some journeys against paid employment and some against freelance and some against capital (*Einkommen aus Kapitalvermögen*).

You can of course entrust the whole bag of tricks to a local accountant but my experience has been that it is better to prepare everything in advance for him merely to check through and adjust. It is much cheaper this way because accountants charge according to the amount of time spent plus a percentage of the sums involved. Ordering the receipts and adding up the different types of expenses yourself saves him time and enables you to see what is going on. Unfortunately the British habit of handing everything over to an accountant and letting him get on with the job does not work. My experience has been that many of the so-called professions are slow, incompetent and — for what they do — too expensive.

Government employees and tax: income tax
Government employees are taxed at source. They pay as they earn. Taxes and other deductions normally amount to about a third of the gross salary. Income is taxed at a basic rate of 22 per cent and then rises to 56 per cent (1990: 19.5 to 53 per cent). This amount of tax can be considerably reduced by subtracting the so-called *Betriebskosten* as mentioned above. Income from dividends and interest is added to salary or wages and taxed accordingly. There is no distinction between earned and unearned income except that dividends are subjected to a special withholding tax of 25 per cent (*Kapitalertragssteuer*) which may

then be subtracted from the total income tax assessment.

Wealth tax (Vermögenssteuer)
Unlike the UK and USA, there is a wealth tax for those taxpayers possessing more than DM 80,000. From this sum may be deducted DM 10,000 held on savings accounts. The rate is levied at 0.5 per cent and the tax is payable every three years. Property is also included, not at its market value but at its assessed value (*Einheitswert*) which is much less. Wealth tax will probably not be a problem for most long stayers, at least at the beginning.

The problem is whether those who possess capital in the UK are liable to German wealth tax. The answer would appear to be 'Yes', except that hitherto German local inland revenue offices do not appear to have been at all interested. However, it is up to the taxpayer to file the wealth tax return (*Vermögenssteuererklärung*) and not for the tax inspector to demand the tax be paid. The problem with investment returns from UK trusts received by beneficiaries resident in Germany is that the British concept of a trust, ie the distinction between legal ownership vested in the trustees as distinct from the beneficiary, is unknown in Germany. What German tax law does recognise is the distinction between a beneficiary receiving only a part of the money due to him or her (the income) as opposed to the capital amount to which the beneficiary may under certain conditions become entitled later on. *Vermögenssteuer* may thus be levied only on income and can be postponed to such time, if ever, that capital is released to the beneficiary. It is very complicated. Get good specialist advice and do some research of your own.

Making a will
Before going abroad you should make a will to establish the domicile of your capital, to have your 'wishes properly expressed' (correct legal parlance) and to choose an executor. A solicitor or bank will advise you. If you should unfortunately die in Germany without having made a will, your relatives become entangled in legal complications, and your own wishes regarding disposal of your money and personal effects (which often carry much trouble afterwards — watches, jewellery, etc) may be restricted or disregarded.

3
The Social Net

Social Services
Very important for the long stayer is the question of social security. Whilst Western Germany is not a welfare state, as in the United Kingdom, it still has many features that resemble the British social system. The organisation is different; health schemes instead of a government health service, an emphasis on State pensions rather than State pensions and private insurance, and a system of graded contributions dependent upon the type of employment as opposed to a universal system of payment. (Insurance goes back to Bismarck's time.) In general, the State does not run its own health service, but supervises public and private health schemes, which also include provision for medical treatment arising from accidents but which are paid for by the relevant State-regulated professional or trade insurance organisation (*Berufsgenossenschaft*). Unemployment and social benefits are paid directly by the State. The State also runs jobs centres and only allows limited scope to private employment agencies. The following is only a rough outline of the services offered, concentrating on those likely to be of interest to foreign visitors. Basically you are concerned with pensions on retirement, accident and health insurance together with unemployment benefit.

First of all, what is the position about continuing contributions to State or private pension schemes at home?

National Insurance Contributions
The most sensible thing to do before moving to Germany is to obtain leaflet SA29 which gives general guidance for those going abroad to work, and supplement this by reading the leaflet dealing with Germany. Basically, if UK employed, you are obliged to continue Class I contributions for the first 12 months of employment in Germany and thereafter you may pay either Class II or Class III contributions or none at all. If German employed you

The Social Net

can opt immediately for Class I. It is normally advisable to pay Class II contributions, which entitle you to sickness and invalid benefit on eventual return to the UK, which Class III does not. The main thing for the future is that these contributions count towards your basic National Insurance retirement pension and where applicable towards a widow's benefit.

Life assurance premiums

Inform your insurance company that you are moving to Germany and pay your premium gross instead of net unless you are a member of the armed forces. If you pay premiums net when they should have been paid gross, the Inland Revenue is empowered to demand payment of the difference, that is, 'claw back' the amount from the policy holder.

The cost

Social insurance (including health) cost 450 thousand million DM in 1980, that is 30 per cent of the social product. Almost 90 per cent of the population (54 million) are insured. *Angestellten* (salaried employees) have to be insured when their regular income is 75 per cent or less of the limit for liability to pay contributions (*Beitragsbemessungsgrenze der Rentenversicherung*) of DM 5,700. Self-employed people are required to do the same. Contributions amount to 18.7 per cent of gross income, the employer and employee each paying half. Those who earn more may insure themselves voluntarily (that is, be *freiwillig versichert*) both for retirement pensions and for health insurance (to be considered later).

The self-employed may either be *pflicht* (obligatorily) or *freiwillig* (voluntarily) insured; if the latter, they pay monthly contributions (from DM 94 up to DM 1,066), but do not receive a pension in case of being unable to work (*Berufs- oder Erwerbsunfähigkeit*).

Pensions

If you ultimately join the German pension scheme your contributions will be calculated as a percentage of your salary, your employer, if you are an *Angestellter* paying half and if a *Beamter* (official) all. Old-age pensioners receive 60–70 per cent of their former salaries. However this is only conceived

The Social Net

as a basic pension to ensure that people have enough to live on. It cannot cover everything, especially not the extras that a pensioner was used to during his working life. At least this is the argument put forward by insurance companies, which try to sell insurance for old-age retirement and in the event of someone becoming an invalid and thus unable to work (*berufsunfähig*). As in any country it is necessary to take great care before selecting a policy. It needs to be tailored to the individual. State employees (*Beamten* and *Angestellten*) are members of the Government Supplementary Insurance Scheme (*Zusatzversicherung*) to be considered later.

Local retirement pensions

Basically there are two types of State pension schemes, those for workers (*Arbeiter*) and those for salaried employees (*Angestellten*), although some differences between the two systems are being done away with. Both systems have their complications but the basic principle remains; the more you pay in, the more you get out with the proviso that how you pay in, and for how long, may well enable you to enjoy a larger pension in the end, at the same time having reduced the amount of your contributions. In other words, the basic principle of the more you pay in, the more you receive in yearly retirement pension does not always hold. Like so many other kinds of dealing with the State, it is an art to get the best deal.

If in doubt, the local State insurance office (*Landesversicherungsanstalt* — LVA for short) will have a list of experts (*Rentenberater*) who will advise you on pension matters for a fee.

Most English-speaking long stayers are likely to be *Angestellten* and here it is important to distinguish between the basic type of State pension for which contributions are payable to the main headquarters in Berlin (*Bundesversicherungsanstalt* — BVA for short) and the supplementary insurance (*Zusatzversicherung*) for civil servants at the *Versorgungsanstalt des Bundes und der Länder* — VBL for short — in Karlsruhe. The paradox is as follows: although an employee (*Angestellter*) pays 18.70 per cent of his gross income (salary) to Berlin and usually less is paid to Karlsruhe (by the employer), in the end it is Karlsruhe that makes up the difference (which may be considerable) between the basic pension and the sum which represents up to 70 per cent (or whatever percentage it is, depending upon length of service, etc.). Generally the lower your final basic Berlin pension is in relation to the ultimate pension you are to receive, the higher your Karlsruhe supplement will be, regardless of the amount your employer paid in on your behalf, which is determined by other factors. Hence the importance of ensuring that your employer registers you for Karlsruhe and pays the contributions. Some employers omit to do this to save paying the contributions, and after a certain time has elapsed it is difficult to have the matter rectified without taking the employer to court.

Health

West Germany does not have a UK-type National Health system, but a system of health insurance schemes, some of which are supervised by the government and others which are privately run but subject to certain legal requirements. Under a certain level of income (*Beitragsbemessungsgrenze* DM 4,275) both workers (*Arbeiter*) and employees (*Angestellten*) are required to be insured (*pflichtversichert*) either with the *AOK* (*Allgemeine Ortskrankenkasse*) or by a supplementary health scheme (*Ersatzkasse*) or to insure themselves with a private insurance scheme. Usually it depends upon the wage or salary; *AOK* is usually for wage earners, *Ersatzkassen* and private insurance organisations for salary earners (*Angestellten*). Members pay only part of the premiums (*Beiträge*), the employer paying 50 per cent. If, however, the wage or salary (*Arbeitsentgelt*) does not reach one tenth of the *Beitragsbemessungsgrenze*, the employer pays the whole premium.

Large companies have their own health insurance schemes. Foreign salary and wage earners must join a public or private scheme. Your monthly contribution is charged at 12.5 per cent of your gross wage or salary. Your employer pays half. If you are privately insured, your employer pays half of your contributions and 50 per cent of medical expenses not covered by the private insurance scheme.

How the system works

As a member of a health insurance scheme (*Krankenkasse*) you receive a booklet or batch of certificates (*Krankenscheine*). One

29

The Social Net

Schein entitles a patient to treatment by a doctor of his or her choice for a quarter of a year. Officially this should be presented when first going to the doctor but may be submitted later. Take great care not to lose or mislay the *Scheine* (they are extremely valuable).

A separate booklet of *Scheine* is available for dental treatment where the same procedure is adopted. With dental treatment, in particular with the provision of certain types of false teeth and the like, the *Krankenkasse* will not pay all of the cost of treatment. The dentist will however make this clear and explain the alternatives. Do not hesitate to go into the matter in detail or to ask him for time to think it over. You can then, if necessary, discuss it with the local office of your *Krankenkasse*, which may be able to suggest a cheaper solution or confirm that the dentist has advised you correctly. Some dentists, mercifully few, are not above suggesting more expensive or extensive treatment than is necessary. Mainly it will be a question of aesthetics in the type of filling or false teeth to be chosen.

The same is true when choosing glasses and frames. There again the *Krankenkasse*, like the NHS, will pay only the basic charges.

If you need to consult a specialist and are confident of what is wrong, there is no need to consult a GP (*Allgemeiner Praktischer Arzt*), although you can obtain a transfer certificate (*Überweisungsschein*), but simply hand the specialist another *Schein*. The only thing you may not do is hand out two *Scheine* to the same type of doctor or specialist during the same quarter. You may, however, change doctor or specialist at the end of the quarter.

On going abroad on holiday, it is advisable to obtain a certificate from the *Krankenkasse* which will entitle you to free medical treatment abroad where there is a reciprocal agreement; for example with the UK government for treatment under the NHS for members of German *Pflichtkassen* (the compulsorily insured). For a UK citizen living in Germany, who visits America, it is advisable to take out a local accident insurance policy for accidents or health illness whilst in the States. Make sure that you carry an English translation of the certificate so that in the (it is hoped) unlikely event of a serious accident or illness, the American hospital staff will understand that you are covered. Local insurance policies available for travel abroad are extremely reasonable — 80 Pfg a day — and it is well worth the peace of mind, but again do not forget the English translation. Most accidents etc, seem to happen over the weekend or on a public holiday when your insurance company cannot be reached to confirm by telex or fax that you are covered.

Health

Everything is based on what Germans call *Solidaritätsprinzip* (share and share alike) whereby members' subscriptions plus their employers' contributions are used for the good of all. The services provided should be regardless of individual premiums, the lower-income employee being treated as well as his better paid colleagues. In practice, however, those who pay more are more demanding and those who pay anything may well demand something, simply because they feel that they are entitled to something for their money.

This of course, was, not the intention of *Solidaritätsprinzip*. If everybody tries to obtain his or her 'moneys worth' in the short-run, little or nothing is left in the long-run; the system goes bankrupt (as it was threatening to do) unless massive increases in contributions are levied; and the element of security for the future goes missing. It is this element of insurance that members are really paying for and they can be sure of obtaining it all the time only by not using the services of the scheme unless absolutely necessary. Hence the need for drastic reform.

Reducing health costs

As with the British NHS, German health schemes have suffered a so-called cost explosion (*Kostenexplosion*), total cost of health and medicine having risen between 1960 and 1987 by 1,300 per cent so that it has become approximately 13 per cent of wages or salaries. The present Minister for Health and Social Welfare, Herr Norbert Blüm, introduced a 'reform' aimed at making medical care more cost effective without reducing the quality of such care. From the beginning of 1989, doctors, dentists and chemists were given a limit which they may not exceed; if the patient insists on a more expensive drug or dentures when other, cheaper, ones would be equally beneficial, he or she must pay the difference. Grants are paid to families looking after sick members at home. Payments are no longer made for transport by taxi unless absolutely necessary. This led to a protest by taxi drivers who found taking patients to hospital for treatment a good source of income. Blüm expects families to help out or for patients to use public transport. As taxis in Germany are usually very expensive the Minister should be able to effect considerable savings.

The worst thing about going to a doctor or specialist as an *AOK* or *Ersatzkasse* patient is the time you may have to wait. Private patients do not usually have to wait so long. As an *Ersatzkasse* patient I must confess that I tend to bully the receptionist if I think my time is being unduly wasted. Save for emergencies, if a practice is efficiently run, it should not be necessary to wait for more than 30 minutes. I always ask the best time to come, which is usually very early or just before the practice closes. If I think I am being messed about and it is a new quarter or there is a new specialist, I refuse to hand over the new *Schein* until I have more or less been shown into the medical man's presence. I feel somewhat guilty afterwards about my bad behaviour but, on the other hand, I feel entitled to ensure that no-one wastes my time.

Private insurance

I have never been a private patient because doctors may legitimately charge what they like. If you can trust the doctor that is fine, but if you are taken seriously ill and have to go to hospital the sky could be the limit. This itself can be limited by being privately insured.

However whilst the private insurance organisations (*Privatkrankenkassen*) offer personal, individual and essential private health care for premiums less than the *Pflichtkassen* (the *AOK* and *Ersatzkassen*), they are more particular about whom they take on healthwise. They pay an agreed amount (*Tagesgeld*) — say DM 100 — daily for the period one is off work through illness or accident (*Krankengeld*). *Pflichtkassen* pay 80 per cent of the last net daily month's salary up to 546 days (78 weeks). Some private insurance companies give their members a card that they show when taken to hospital. It looks and is like a credit card. The hospital then knows which organisation to bill and what services are covered by the issuer.

The Social Net

It makes sense to join the public *AOK* or *Ersatzkassen* which will cover the main expenses, and then take out a supplementary policy with a private insurance organisation which will pay for a single room in a hospital and entitles the patient to a choice of surgeon in the event of an operation. Such an additional policy costs more than £200 per annum and is tax deductible as are the contributions to the public health schemes, up to a certain amount covering health and insurance payments.

Chronic illnesses
Parents with children suffering from illness such as diabetes, epilepsy or haemophilia can be assured of the most modern treatment available under the local health insurance schemes. The same holds for those members of the family who may be suffering from depression or mental illnesses.

Cancer
Unfortunately cancer, after heart disease, is one of the most significant causes of death in the Federal Republic. Great efforts are made by the government and by the *Krankenkassen* to encourage people to have themselves examined regularly to catch the disease at an early stage when cure is possible. Such examinations are free and the relevant *Schein* (certificate) is included in the batch of certificates which the *Krankenkassen* gives their members.

Unemployment benefit
Before considering unemployment benefit, a word of warning — 'No dole for strikers!'. The main point, as far as a long stayer is concerned, is that German social welfare services — for which some long stayers are eligible — are on the whole generous. By comparison with the UK, there is an important difference; the family of a worker on strike cannot claim the dole (*Arbeitslosengeld*). Here the German work ethic is involved. You have to work to live, which doesn't mean to say there are no skivers. There are. Moonlighting is also a problem. But by and large, Germans accept the responsibility of paying for their own families and the State is not called upon to help out to the extent that it is in UK during strikes. One could sum up by saying that the State is basically there to help people to help themselves.

The Social Net

All this is unlikely to concern the long stayer, but it might in the case of losing one's job, or getting the sack. It can happen to anyone and it is in such a situation that, as a foreigner, one feels especially vulnerable. If there is a family to support, no private means, modest local savings, a house but no job, life can look very grim indeed.

Getting the sack

A few rules might help at this stage and will show how the system works. First of all do *not* despair. You may only think you have lost your job. No-one may be dismissed without the works council (*Betriebsrat*) being consulted. The only exception is a university where academic staff can be dismissed without the *Betriebsrat* being heard. Whilst the *Betriebsrat* cannot insist on reinstatement or stop dismissal, it can steer the issue in the employee's favour and, if necessary, obtain legal advice and assistance in the Labour Court. The Labour Court *can* insist on re-instatement and sometimes does, or it can award compensation if it is of the opinion that the dismissal was unjustified but does not feel re-instatement is the right solution. So dismissal may not necessarily be final.

If you become unemployed after 6 months and have paid contributions to the *Arbeitslosenversicherung* (unemployment insurance), you are entitled to 62 or 68 per cent of your net salary, depending upon whether or not you have children, up to a period of 32 months depending upon your age. During this period you must be prepared to take a job roughly equivalent to the one you have lost. If you turn down a reasonable offer for no good reason, unemployment payments cease. You may not simply receive unemployment benefit and then return home as some people do. If *Arbeitslosengeld* (unemployment benefit) runs out without your having obtained employment, you will no longer receive unemployment benefit but will become eligible for unemployment assistance (*Arbeitslosenhilfe*) that is 56 or 58 per cent of your former salary again depending upon whether or not you have children; this continues indefinitely and can be supplemented by additional payments for rent (*Wohngeld*), clothes, etc.

4
Education

Education: the child's choice too

Whether or not to educate your children in Germany is not just a decision for you but for the children concerned, because it affects their happiness and academic progress. Before — it seems centuries ago — children were 'to be seen and not heard' but not so today. The situation is complicated by whether the decision will be seen to be right in twenty years time. Will the European Community live up to expectations? Is a young person better off with a German, ie, European continental education rather than a traditional American or British, be it an Independent or a State school? These questions are imponderables on their own. Children view things from a more practical point of view: fears, loss of friends, difficulty in making new ones in a foreign language (assuming that no German is known).

International schools

A possible solution to the problem of whether or not to leave children at British schools or try and effect the transition to German schools is the so-called international school which aims to provide an American, British or even French education up to American High School Diploma, GCE 'O' and 'A' levels (viz the recent equivalents) and the International Baccalaureate in a local German environment. There are three international schools in Hamburg, Frankfurt and Munich which provide a bilingual syllabus. The language of instruction is English, though of course provision is made to teach English as a second language to non-native speakers. As those attending co-ed international schools are usually children of well heeled parents or parents working for firms or government organisations providing educational subsidies, the schools are usually in pleasant surroundings and the facilities — accommodation if boarding — and food are of high standard. Sport, art and cultural facilities are excellent and due attention is paid to

Education

providing science laboratories and libraries, etc. Great care is taken to employ only properly experienced and qualified teaching staff.

The problem, if it is one, may be the blending of different national educational requirements and, though this may seem a contradiction, having English as the medium of instruction where some of the staff may not in fact be native speakers. Though international schools can point to excellent examination results for some pupils, it may be that other children are less successful which is of course natural in any school. No doubt international schools suit some pupils and not others, and this is where specialist advice should be taken either at home with an independent organisation like Gabitas Thring Educational Trust and or at the school concerned. With increased demand for this type of education, honest and objective advice can be expected.

Army children (American and British) can attend local schools, about the quality of which it is difficult to generalise. Some seem perfectly adequate, others less so, but it depends upon the needs of the particular child. The main advantage is that the child is near home; the question is, to what extent does the education offered match the educational requirements of the home country? Undoubtedly the best course of action is to take specialist advice and visit the school in question before making a decision. If you move a lot and educate your children abroad so they are educated at a variety of schools, the continuity may be lost. This can be overcome by UK, ie home-based education.

Local education: in detail
Education is free to every child and is provided by the State. It is organised into *Kindergarten, Volksschule (Grundschule)*, age 6–13, *Hauptschule*, age 12–14, with *Hauptschulabschluß* as the final exam followed by trade school *(Berufsschule)*, age 15–18, for future manual workers: mechanics, hairdressers, shop assistants, etc; *Realschule* (12–15) with the final exam of *Mittlere Reife* for the middle ranks of commerce (bank clerks, junior officials and executives); and *Gymnasien* for the most gifted who are able to sit *Abitur* ('A' level or High School Diploma). There are four types of German grammar school: humanistic *(humanistische)* with an emphasis on the classics

Education

— Latin and Greek; *musische* with an emphasis on music and art; *wirtschaftliche* with an emphasis on modern economics; and *neusprachliche* where modern languages are taught. As in America and other English-speaking countries, fewer pupils are learning Latin and Greek and the classical grammar schools have fallen on hard times. As Friedrich Nietzsche, who around 1870 taught in Greek in Basel said: 'Dem Menschen wird nur so viel Kultur gestattet, als im Interesse des Erwerbs ist, aber so viel auch von ihm gefordert' (People will only be allowed to learn as much culture as it is in the interest of business to do so, but also as much as will be demanded of them). A reform that has been introduced is an intensive course in a special subject (*Leistungskurs*) which involves writing a paper (*Facharbeit*). The intention of such a course is to provide a bridge to university as part of the preparation for *Abitur*.

Whilst *Abitur* gives the constitutional right to attend university, it does not entitle the *Abiturient* to read all subjects. So-called *numerus clausus* (a restriction on the numbers admitted to a particular subject) applies to medicine, veterinary medicine and dentistry. Only those with the best marks in *Abitur* are taken.

This is a short description of the conventional traditional education system. There is however also the so-called *Zweiter Bildungsweg* (adult education) for those who for one reason or another left school, took a job and then resumed their education in their free time. The structure of this system includes the *Berufsschule* (trade school) for apprentices and those wanting to resume their education but lacking qualifications to attend the next school up the ladder (the *Berufsaufbauschule*, equivalent to junior technical college). In this latter school the *Fachabitur*, that is a more practically orientated *Abitur*, can be sat for, which if passed entitles the student to attend the *Fachhochschule*, equivalent to a polytechnic or technical college.

As far as the long stayer is concerned, there are also *Volkshochschulen* (adult educational colleges) open to everybody, where courses are held in most subjects. It is also possible to take exams. Germans often study foreign languages there and use the occasion as a means of meeting like-minded people.

Education

When deciding whether or not to have your children educated in Germany it is as well to know how the average educated German views the subject.

In Germany State education is accepted to be the best available. It is the preserve of the *Länder* governments and is regarded by everybody as the key to success in the future for children, talented and less talented alike but often with equally motivated and ambitious parents. Court cases are pursued with great acrimony against the different ministries of education to appeal marks, grades, examination results and anything that could be seen to have held up a particular student's progress to the top. Education is considered the great meal ticket for those who can excel, that is until recently when unemployment made severe inroads into the ranks of highly qualified graduates, especially teachers. Whole university faculties have been virtually decimated and students have switched from the arts, which they usually studied to teach in school, to bread-and-butter subjects such as business studies, which hold out the best prospect of a job in industry.

This may appear to be a very crude introduction to German education, but it is, with some qualifications, true. If you want to educate your children in Germany, then you are becoming associated with a particular school atmosphere. What is offered at school is an excellent grounding in basic subjects, acknowledged as better than in UK, but at the end, a preparation for university. This means relatively early specialisation, felt by some pedagogues to be too early academically within the local system. Viewed internationally, Germans tend to leave both school and university later than in English-speaking countries viz, school between 18 and 19 and university between 26 and 28 years of age depending upon the subject studied. It has now been recognised that with the coming of the Common Market in 1992, German graduates will be at a disadvantage *vis-à-vis* their younger European colleagues. Attempts are now being made to encourage students to shorten their studies. However this is proving difficult because of the existing structure of university education which is often highly theoretical and specialised.

Parents thinking of sending their children to local schools should take this into consideration. A German education is excellent, but it might prove to be self-defeating in the end so

Education

far as future employment in Germany is concerned. People now recognise that the main problem in the future is likely to be getting a job; there are some highly educated out-of-work doctors and teachers; the social problems are immense. Undoubtedly it pays to think at least a decade in advance.

All this assumes that an English or American child can be transplanted to a German school and can overcome the problem of language, which should not be underestimated. This depends on the age of the child, its ability to pick up German quickly enough to perform well at school and whether or not the effort involved will interfere with the standard of education already reached at home. The importance of learning the language is a subject to which I shall return in this book.

There are, of course, private language schools that cater for the needs of newcomers and there is a library full of language courses on video and audio cassettes. Moreover, private tuition is readily available in most towns. University students are cheaper than professional teachers but not so skilled. The best way to learn a language is to talk with local children. The teacher can impart the rudiments of grammar, other children teach the idioms. Learning a foreign language is not easy, especially German which, to use correctly, does require a thorough grounding in grammar. German is a very grammar-orientated language because it is inflected, eg *der alte Mann* (the old man) *gab* (gave) *dem jungen Mann* (the young man) *einen guten Füllhalter* (a good fountain pen).

However, it is possible to acquire a smattering which will enable one to get by at the beginning before becoming more proficient at the language — see Chapter 10 *The Language*.

Elternbeirat (*parents' council*)

German schools are usually aware of their responsibility to the parents as well as to the children, though the extent to which this is apparent will vary from school to school depending upon the headmaster (*Schulleiter*) and staff. There are parents' evenings (*Elternabende*) where parents can meet each other and teachers have *Sprechstunden* (consultation hours) for parents. You should attend them if there is any question that you would like to raise with the teacher about your child. Obviously some teachers are more forthcoming than others, but on the whole

Education

you can assume that teachers will be as helpful as possible within the time limit set by their many responsibilities. As far as complaints are concerned, it is always as well to be very sure of your ground first.

If you are dissatisfied with the progress your child is making at school it is much better to approach the teacher and ask for advice first rather than begin with a complaint. You want the teacher's help in the first instance. If this is not forthcoming, you can then change tack. As a foreigner you will in any case be very dependent upon the teacher's goodwill.

It is surprising how often *simple* things can count so much. Pupils or students who cannot see or hear very well often sit at the back of the class. If they sat in the front, it would be easier, but they become used to a certain degree of isolation through their disability and do not want to draw attention to themselves by sitting in front, which is, of course, what they should do to improve their performance. It is essential to have a child's hearing and sight checked regularly, which naturally should be optimal when instruction is carried out in a foreign language.

Finally there is an *Elternbeirat* (parent's council) in every school and this acts in an advisory and support capacity to the *Schulleiter* (head teacher).

The truism that a good education is the key to success has today become questionable, especially in Germany where there are so many unemployed intellectuals. The key to success is no longer a good academic education, but the *right* education to find a job.

5
Transport

Introduction
Getting about can be a major problem if public transport is thin on the ground. In any case the motor car, as in other European countries, is very much a part of everyday life.

This section in 'preparations' is the first to suggest movement and therefore serves as a transition between preparations in theory and the move in practice.

The motor car
The average German's dedication to his or her motor car varies according to age and income group; some Germans spend every available free moment, cleaning, repairing or driving it; others regard it purely and simply as a means of getting from A to B. Accident statistics, especially the horrific pile-ups on the motorways (*Autobahnen*), and environmental problems (dying forests, crumbling public buildings in the cities together with the increased toxic content in the air), have caused the government and people to take another look at the disadvantages as well as the advantages of general motorisation.

Whatever is said against the automobile, as far as accidents and the environment are concerned, German industry is to a great extent dependent upon continued production of motor cars especially in the export market. As with the production of armaments it is difficult to opt out of automobile production even if you wanted to, though it is realised that home consumption is reaching saturation point and demand is likely to level off in the future. Cities such as Munich have, in any case, so far as traffic is concerned, reached saturation point.

This short introduction should not dissuade the long stayer from bringing his or her car to Germany. On the contrary, if you live in the country or in the suburbs, it may be the only practical means of transport; if you are a single person, it may be

Transport

the only way of getting out of your flat in a small town to explore the countryside if you have neither the time nor inclination to do so by bike.

You must decide whether to sell your English car (if American, presumably you would hesitate to ship your car over the ocean) and invest in a German one or keep your own car and risk problems in servicing and possible difficulties in getting a reasonable price when you come to resell it. In my experience German cars are infinitely superior to English ones as far as reliability and performance are concerned. Moreover German restrictions and regulations regarding toxic exhaust, in particular the fitting of catalytic convertors, make it sensible to buy a local car.

Keeping your own car

If, despite this advice, you do decide to keep your own car, it is obviously simplest to drive it to Germany either using the Dover–Calais ferry and passing through France and Belgium to the German border or taking the Dover–Ostend crossing and simply continuing through Belgium. The former is a much shorter crossing than the latter, but it entails a longer drive with a sometimes poorly signposted route (although the newly opened motorway from the outskirts of Calais to Paris now affords the motorist a faster time to Liège and from there to the German border). Tolls are charged, so it is advisable to have some French money with you, which can also be used for *Services*. If going Dover–Calais, it pays to ask for a route from the AA or RAC.

If you bring your car from farther afield, it will obviously have to be shipped. Americans can, however, order a German car and pay for it in the US and then take delivery in Germany thus saving money. Otherwise to ship a middle-sized car from Los Angeles costs between $700 and 900 and from New York $600 to 700. Foreign cars become liable for local road tax after one year when the car has to be inspected by TÜV (*Technischer Überwachungsverein*). As American, particularly Californian, anti-toxic regulations are stricter than German, no difficulty should be experienced on this score. With British cars, it is a different matter. Here advice should be sought from the manufacturer or your automobile club.

Transport

Buying a car
Whilst buying a new car is simple provided you can pay for it, trading in your old car in Germany can present difficulties if it is not a German left-hand-drive car and if it does not meet local safety and environmental regulations (with the German equivalent of MOT, *TÜV* which is much stricter than MOT). The dealer might try to insist that you have the necessary changes made before he accepts the car. Do not agree to this. Having the car converted may cost a small fortune and no little time. Try another dealer.

Buying a secondhand car
If buying a new car is too expensive when settling in, you might well consider purchasing a secondhand car. The risks are manifold as at home and redress is not easy. There is no German equivalent of the Office of Fair Trading or the Consumer Affairs Division of the Department of Trade which has any teeth in a situation like this. A private contract gives one the best chance of obtaining satisfaction from the courts. If you buy from a private person, who sells his or her car from home, or from the premises of a garage, be very careful indeed. Even if the seller has been recommended by friends, you should take great care not only over the mechanical condition of the car, examining underneath for rust etc, but also concerning the paperwork.

One does not just hand over the money and drive away but usually is required to sign a *Kaufvertrag* (contract — see illustration) which usually states that the buyer has test driven the car (*Probefahrt*), which has not had an accident (*Unfallfrei*), has a certain number of kilometers on the clock (*Kilometerstand*) — the veracity of which is very difficult to check, and — most important — that the seller accepts no responsibility for the state of the car (as seen) and test driven (*wie besichtigt*).

So please examine the car minutely and if you do not understand anything about cars, take along someone who does. Do not, if you are uncertain about anything, accept any verbal assurances about putting anything right, if it goes wrong, without having such an assurance added in writing to the contract. If you have a witness, this should suffice, but it is still better to have it in writing. Finally, do not hand over any money until you *have* test driven the car, examined it thoroughly and the

Transport

log book (*Kraftfahrzeugbrief*) too and compared the name written therein with the seller's Identity Card (*Ausweis*) to see that the person selling you the car is in fact the owner. Examine the number plate of the car at the back to see whether the small coloured plaque is still valid (see illustration). It will show when the next MOT (*TÜV*) is due. If the inspection plaque is no longer valid, there could be something very expensive wrong with the car; and, if the plaque is out of date, the vehicle should not be on the road. Finally, if all this is in order, it is essential to have insurance arranged before you drive away.

These are, of course, all obvious things, except possibly taking the paperwork seriously because there are cases of thieves selling cars. Obviously you must be even more careful at local car auctions. You should also be especially careful, when buying a secondhand car that has been traded in, that the person selling it to you is not claiming to do so on commission, in which case he will style himself in the contract as an *Autoagentur* (agent). This usually means that if anything goes wrong with the car, he will try and wriggle out of any responsibility because he is not the seller but only the intermediary. This is often a trick to avoid paying VAT (*Mehrwertsteuer*). The legal responsibility of intermediaries is less stringent than that of sellers. At least that will be his argument.

Driving licence

A British or American driving licence is valid in the Federal Republic for a year from the date of entry. Thereafter, a local one has to have been obtained (no test is necessary). Don't wait too long to obtain a German licence from the *Führerscheinstelle* (driving licence office) or you may be required to take the full test (practical and theoretical) or, worse still, face a prison sentence if caught on the road without a licence by the police. If the driving licence is not valid and there is an accident, no German insurance company will pay a cent.

Driving Insurance

If you are going to stay in Germany for a long time, it is as well to obtain local insurance. (You cannot legally drive your privately owned vehicle without it. Third party liability insurance is mandatory.) You will, unless on government service, no

Transport

doubt be obliged to because home insurance companies do not normally extend their insurance of cars for periods abroad of longer than 6 months. If, for any reason, you are allowed to retain a home number plate (which normally has to be exchanged for a German one within 12 months from date of entry), then only one major insurance company in Germany would insure the car (*Albingia* in Hamburg, which belongs to the Guardian Royal Exchange Insurance [UK] Ltd in London but which has district branch offices and agents throughout Germany). Those on government service — including members of HM Forces — now have normal UK number plates for security purposes. If you do not belong to this category it is as well to make full enquiries at the local branch of the *Allgemeiner Deutscher Automobilclub* (ADAC for short).

The cost of driving a car in Germany

ADAC publishes regularly in its journal the average cost of running different makes and types of car. According to this you can work out how much it costs per kilometre to run and, most important of all, how much you need to save every month to replace the car after three or four years.

Driving in Germany is faster and more dangerous than at home. It is as well to familiarise yourself with the traffic signs and of course with driving on the right instead of the left as in the UK. You will soon realise after driving for a short time in Germany that there is a different psychology involved. Local drivers can become very impatient and aggressive, though they usually make allowances for foreigners. The cardinal rule is that traffic coming from the right has priority unless it is changing from a secondary to a major road.

The police

Foreigners will usually find the police most helpful and will have nothing to fear from them. It is however as well to understand that in Germany the police have what the locals call a *Kontrollfunktion* — they are there essentially to see that people obey the law. The police do not necessarily have a very good image with the public. There are historical reasons for this. Young people often refer to the police as *Bullen* (bulls). In general the police, while they are sometimes rather ham-fisted

45

with demonstrators, suffer a lot of provocation for which their training and education do not always fit them. However, law-abiding English-speaking visitors will usually find the police as helpful as could be.

Offences: fines

The great distinction between Germany and Britain is that the German police are empowered to levy semi fines (called *Verwarnungen*) or actual fines (*Bußen*) on the spot or after the event by post, whereas the British police are not. In Germany the police have certain summary jurisdiction not accorded to their British or American colleagues, although in Germany as in UK you can appeal to the courts.

If you appeal in Germany against a ticket for a parking or speeding offence you may well have the original fine increased as well as additional court expenses to pay. It is better to pay up. However, if you believe a mistake has been made, then going to court, with all its risks and inconveniences, may be the wisest course. You should not be fooled by the delay in being mailed the demand to pay the fine after the original offence has been reported or after speeding has been registered by camera in a speed trap. It may take months to be called to account. Sometimes you are sent the actual photos, sometimes not. There are also cameras set up at traffic lights to record those who drive through on red.

Traffic signs

German traffic signs are, as far as possible, international but there are a few local ones which are well worth learning, eg *einfädeln* — which is when one row of traffic merges with another. This is simple enough in the open country at the brow of a hill when two lanes on the right or left merge into one to avoid overtaking at this juncture. What is less simple, and may suddenly occur in town is where a street narrows after a cross roads and the right hand lane merges into the middle right hand lane. If you do not watch out you may end up on the pavement.

The essential thing is always to remember that German drivers know the rules and expect others to do the same. If they have right of way, they take it regardless. This is not because they

Transport

mean to be inconsiderate but because they are programmed to expect everyone to drive by the rule book.

German trains

Travel by train, especially by Intercity (IC) and Intercity Experimental (ICI) is extremely comfortable. Trains run on a wide gauge track which together with excellent suspension affords a smooth ride. Trains are also kept clean and are seldom vandalised. They are also kept in a good state of repair. The cost, first-class, is 31.5 Pfg per kilometer, and second class 21 Pfg a kilometer for distances over 100 kilometers. There are also different types of cheaper tickets, weekend excursion offers, especially for senior citizens and the like, which makes travel by train appreciably cheaper. British old age pensioners can avail themselves of the Senior Citizen Rail Card and a Rail Europe Senior Card which enable them to obtain approximately a 40 per cent reduction on travel in the Federal Republic. Young travellers under 26 on a visit can obtain Interrail Cards for £139, providing a month's unlimited travel within Europe including West Germany.

Weekend breaks including *Städtetouren* (excursions to different cities) with accommodation included are well worth trying if you want to have a rest from driving. Most of the larger or middle-sized stations have an enquiries section (*Auskunft*) which has a whole array of free explanatory brochures. Most of the officials speak some English, at least enough to give advice to prospective travellers. Luggage can be sent in advance, as well as being picked up from home and delivered to your destination hotel or private quarters.

It may take some time getting used to German stations (*Bahnhöfe*) and the way the railway system works. Stations are often fairly central. There are no platform tickets or if there are no-one bothers, at least not on the smaller stations; and on the larger stations no-one collects or checks tickets from arriving passengers. This is all done by the guard on the train.

Railway officials often wear splendid uniforms especially the official who blows the whistle and indicates to the driver the time of departure. He wears a red sash, a red cap and carries a baton (*Befehlsstab*). You almost expect him to burst into a song like a figure in a comic opera. He is, in my experience,

Transport

extremely understanding in holding a train up to let foreign passengers board the train at the last moment! Germans are better organised and seldom late.

Once aboard you enter another world, clean and relaxing and insulated from noise. Take plenty to read, a Thermos flask and sandwiches to economise; snacks are expensive; sit back and enjoy it. The Federal Railways' safety record is second to none, except, one has to add (and this is more intended as a word of warning to the motorist), on branch lines over level crossings. Level crossings are dangerous in any country.

6
The Move and Accommodation

Now for the move itself; getting there from afar can only be by air or sea and is largely a question of time and money. Most people fly and leave transporting effects to a removals' firm. If you have to pay your own fare, shopping around might enable you to find a cheaper one. Crossing the English Channel is relatively uncomplicated yet sometimes tiring and time-consuming by boat. It is relatively speaking expensive for the single person travelling by car. Flying is usually cheaper and less of a hassle. Now for the effects:

Removals
Removals from the UK are trouble-free so long as you employ an experienced removals' firm such as *Pickfords*' in UK and *Mayflower* in the USA (see yellow pages), which is familiar with the job of taking furniture and personal effects to Germany and does it often enough that you won't have to wait too long for delivery. The companies collect small loads and take them to the depot preparatory to sending truck loads routed to different destinations in Europe. The larger the firm, the more frequently it is likely to effect delivery and the quicker this is likely to be in your case. Pickfords requires a copy of your rental agreement to prove that you do have an address for delivery of your effects.

You are well advised to insure effects against loss, theft or fire and especially to read the small print in the insurance form. Insurance companies are not above trying to escape responsibility by strict interpretation of the small print. Should this happen, never take 'no' for an answer from junior executives, but complain direct to the chairman of the board of directors whose name usually appears printed right at the bottom of the company's stationery. You will then usually get satisfaction. Whilst the removals' men appreciate a gratuity, there is no need to spoil them because sometimes their method of dragging rather than lifting furniture has to be seen to be believed.

The Move and Accommodation

Should you decide to keep your British car after all, take the silver and other valuables with you in the car rather than consigning them to the removals' firm.

Customs

On entering the Federal Republic, as when entering the UK, certain goods are forbidden or admitted only under certain conditions: drugs, weapons and munitions; meat and meat products, plants and animals. This is obvious. At the point of entry there are usually the green and red lanes for travellers with nothing or something to declare respectively. There are the usual quantitive restrictions (for those coming from outside Europe) on tobacco (400 cigarettes or 200 cigarillos or 100 cigars or 500g of tobacco). For those living within the Common Market the amounts are reduced to 300 cigarettes, 150 cigarillos or 75 cigars or 400g of tobacco. Common Market citizens are allowed to import 1.5l of spirits with not more than 22% alcohol, 3l of wine of the same alcohol content, 3l of *Schaumwein* or liqueur (*Likörwein*) and 5l of ordinary wine. For those from further afield the relevant amounts are reduced to 1, 2,2 and 2l respectively. Common Market citizens may import 100g of coffee or 400g of coffee essence, others 500 and 200g respectively. Tea is even more restricted: 200g for Common Market citizens, 100g for others. 75g of perfume may be imported by those from the Common Market and only 50g by those from outside. The total value of new goods imported should not exceed DM 400. Usually German customs officers are not very strict or likely to make difficulties. At one time they were concerned with imports of tea and coffee which were then much more expensive in Germany than in England.

For long stayers employing the services of a removals firm the latter will deal with customs. There should be no trouble with household goods.

Housing/accommodation — choice between living in the country or in the town

The main choice is obviously between living in the town or in the country. Living in the country may have aesthetic attractions but it may be far more difficult to feel at home there. This is not because people in the country are any less friendly than in the

The Move and Accommodation

town, quite the reverse, but rural communities tend to be more closely knit and if you do not speak the language, it could prove difficult to become integrated into the community. There is also less sophistication and culture. Those who are used to living in the country might still find German country life preferable to city living.

One important consideration, however, is that the winter in Germany can be far more severe than at home. Driving to work is no fun and can be something of a hazard. Public transport is sparse in some country districts, so that travelling to work can be a problem even though the overall distance to be covered is not very great — see *Transport*.

An important consideration when living in the country is the significance attached to religion in a village. Great store is still attached to going to church.

Undoubtedly a great advantage of living in the country is that there is usually plenty of room for the children and for family pets, especially dogs. You are not living on top of others who might object to family noise or to spare-time pursuits, like woodwork, which often entail disturbing the neighbours.

A town dweller from England may find that life in the country in Germany is even more of a culture shock than expected. Social life tends to centre around village societies and clubs (*Vereine*) devoted to song and sport. Unless you share these particular interests and have a fair knowledge of the language, not to mention the regional dialect, it might be difficult to join in.

One imagines, living in a town, that life in the country is much quieter than in the town, even idyllic. This is not always the case; animal noises may not be disturbing, but the sounds of tractors and hacksaws are. German farms tend to be tidy and clean, but the usual smells and flies abound.

If you are an out-and-out country dweller, all this can be taken in its stride. You need not necessarily be fully integrated into the local community but can enjoy the countryside for its own sake. However, the German rural landscape is not like the British (see illustrations). There is, for example, no equivalent of East Sussex or Somerset country lanes, what George Orwell referred to as the gentle English countryside; it is not soft and intimate, but, especially in the north, can be flat and monotonous with pine tree forests that go on for mile after mile and begin to pall after

51

The Move and Accommodation

a time. The Black Forest (*Schwarzwald*) in the south-west and the remarkable rock formations in the *Fränkische Schweiz* in Upper Franconia together with the beautiful countryside and majestic mountains in Upper Bavaria are of great scenic beauty, but might be more suitable for holidays than for permanent residence.

Life in town

Assuming your place of work is in a town, then it might well be sensible to consider beginning your long stay in Germany by simply renting flat accommodation before taking the more expensive step of renting or buying a house. A flat will usually be less expensive but will offer less room.

Rents depend upon the district. Obviously the larger cities are more expensive than the smaller ones and living in Munich is the most expensive of all because of that city's attractions and proximity to the mountains for holidays and skiing. Normally you rent unfurnished accommodation, though fitted wall-to-wall carpets and a semi- or fully equipped kitchen are provided.

Obviously it will also depend to a great extent upon the size of your family and the amount of furniture you possess as to the size — number of rooms — required. Space is very much at a premium in the cities and small flats can become claustrophobic. Moreover, the nature of the district is important too, just as it would be in London. To what extent, at least to begin with, are you prepared to compromise, to give up what you are used to at home for the settling in period? It also depends on how much, if any, financial assistance you receive from your employer, if not for actually buying property, then perhaps for buying furniture, be it an outright subsidy or a low-interest loan.

Houses

German houses and blocks of flats will always have an entry outside for the fire services, and signs warn motorists not to block this entrance with their vehicles. There is always a hard surface laid down, which in time becomes covered with grass but can still be used by the fire brigade. The path is indicated by wooden pegs driven into the ground.

It is well worth noting that in narrow streets badly parked cars can hinder the fire brigade's arrival at the scene of a fire.

The Move and Accommodation

Always be careful how and where you park your car. Careless parking could cost someone's life by delaying rescue attempts. Local authorities and the *Länder* (state regional authorities) are now experimenting with a new (for Germany) standard system of housing people in rows of 2-storey flats similar to so-called *Reihenhäuser*, semi-detached houses, and are thus an attempt to get away from the block-of-flats' approach. This works better in country districts where land is less expensive.

Rented accommodation

Renting accommodation can be a matter of luck. You are happy with the flat, the rent is right, the landlord accommodating and the neighbours pleasant. You might find it through an advert in the local paper or through a *Makler* (estate agent or realtor). The former is cheap, but can be time-consuming; the latter usually charges two months' rent, but can be quick. Equally the newspaper advert could lead you to an agreeable flat immediately. Usually, in a city like Munich, the desirable flat is gone before you get there and you must resign yourself to innumerable phone calls and an odyssey of viewing different places. Equally too the *Makler* could be a crook (no exaggeration!) and if not that, completely useless. The following advice is therefore offered to those venturing onto the German market without previous experience and with little or no German.

First, try and get local help, some nice German *cognoscente* to advise. Offer a celebratory meal as an inducement (though this will probably not be necessary) to negotiate for you over the phone with both *Makler* and landlord. It should be possible to reduce the number of *Makler* and ultimately the number of flats down to a few.

Certain precautions are worth taking. They may be summed up by the dictum: 'never sign anything without reading it' and if you do not understand it, then have someone explain the relevant document, be it a contract with the *Makler* or the landlord, to you. This advice holds for any business done in Germany. It is always the written word that counts and not the verbal assurances which are so difficult afterwards to have verified. Never be in a hurry to sign whatever anyone tells you. Few offers are unique.

The *Makler* may not charge a fee for work preparatory to

The Move and Accommodation

finding your accommodation. You pay him after he has found you something and not before.

Do *not* sign the contract with the landlord until you have understood every word of it. You don't have to have a written contract, but one is usual. If there is a clause in it you disapprove of, cross it out, for example, how much notice you have to give to leave. Notice usually has to be given in writing some weeks *before* the 3-month period of notice, which extends the period of notice accordingly.

Make sure you know what type of rent you are paying: *Inklusiv*, that is, all included; or so-called *Kaltmiete* (basic rent) plus the *Pauschale* (lump sum) which makes the rent *Warmmiete*. The former excludes, the latter includes monthly payments for services in particular heating and is averaged out over and then calculated for the year as a whole. At the end if you have used more heating than covered by the *Pauschale*, you are presented with an extra bill; if less, you are given a rebate (— see *Gas and electricity*, p61).

Furniture
Buying furniture in Germany can be an expensive business and you may have to get used to a different style of design: *Biedermeier*, even Baroque or Bavarian-Alpine country style. There is some cheap pseudo-antique Italian and Spanish furniture on the market which looks ornate but inside, at the back of the drawers, is slipshod workmanship. One of my colleagues had to stick the back of the drawer to the sides with sticky tape!

If you have furniture at home in reasonable condition, then it is certainly worth bringing over with you and paying the removals' charge. If it is good antique English then it is definitely still an investment, because such furniture is eagerly sought after in Germany. Take specialist advice over this because central heating might cause the veneer to warp or the wood itself to split.

The problem with some English furniture, say repro 1890's style, is that it is difficult to fit it into modern German flats which have relatively low ceilings. This makes it difficult with lamp fittings, which are a confounded nuisance if they hang too low, and look ridiculous if they are fitted flush with the ceiling.

Germans have the same problem with their own drawing room

The Move and Accommodation

lamps, which tend to hang low over the main table. Many is the time that I have got up from the coffee table to say good-bye and hit my head a resounding crack on the lamp above. In time you learn to rise from your seat like a snake ducking gracefully at the same time to avoid the lamp shade.

Carpets are obtainable in all shapes, sizes and price levels. Many Persian, Indian, Pakistani and Nepales, even Moroccan (Bedouin) carpets are available on the market. Germany is conveniently situated for easy access to the carpet making countries. The refugees from Iran and close connections with Turkey have greatly increased the supply of carpets on the German market.

One thing that should not be forgotten is security. Theft is not so prevalent in Germany as in England. People are security conscious and forever, as explained above, locking doors. In any case they are cautious, even suspicious, of strangers. All this helps security. However, being on the continent and with a large immigrant population, there are gangs that specialise in house robberies and seem to be able to send their loot over the frontier in no time.

Particularly worrying is the theft of cars, a third of which, it is reckoned by the police, are taken abroad and resold there.

Valuable possessions are not only a pleasure but have become something of a liability too. You should consider very carefully whether it is worth investing in easily stolen goods such as carpets, pictures, silver etc. You can insure them of course but replacements are never quite the same.

Don't worry if you cannot find every item of furniture locally. There are always relatively cheap weekend flights to London where excellent curtain material, lamps and items of old furniture are obtainable. It is surprising how much you can take back to Germany on a plane (officially up to 400 DM [£120] worth) and how understanding customs officials are; or by a car where no-one bothers to look.

One important note on customs duty; officially duty is not charged on many goods, merely the German Value Added Tax (*Mehrwertsteuer*) which, over a certain sum for the article in question, has been deducted at home. Supposing you bought a coat for £250 on which 15 per cent was paid. If you want to avoid paying VAT the seller will give you a form to be stamped by

55

The Move and Accommodation

German Customs on arrival and then returned to the seller for signature and forwarding to the customs for a refund of VAT. However, if you do this, the German Customs will levy local VAT (*Mehrwertsteuer*) which amounts to the same or more, plus a waste of time at the end of the journey. It is usually not worth it.

Curtains
Many Germans dispense with curtains (*Vorhänge*) as such and just use *Stores* (net curtains) or they may have curtains with either no *Stores* or have a special backing material on the reverse of the curtain. The only problem with the latter is that this material can shrink when the curtain is cleaned, thus spoiling the shape of the curtain.

German duvets and chairs
A German student of mine said that getting into an English bed was like getting inside an envelope, she wasn't used to blankets. Conversely I used to find that German duvets (*Plumos*) always slipped off during the night. They also require great manual dexterity to put the large bolster type contraption inside and then smooth the whole thing down. How hotel chamber maids manage I can't image.

English grandfather chairs, especially the English and American wing-back kind, are rarely used in German living rooms. Much modern German furniture is short backed so there is little support for the back, and can, in my opinion, lead to back trouble.

Neatness and orderliness
Neatness in personal habit also finds expression in neatness and orderliness of design. There seems to be a gadget for everything. This is especially evident in office material and equipment where everything is neat and well thought out.

Most German households own washing machines, and blocks of flats have communal ones. This makes housework much simpler. A large ironing machine (*Heißmangel*) is available to deal with sheets, towels and clothes, and the use of drip-dry shirts saves an incredible amount of time at the ironing board.

Laundries are thorough, wash whiter than white, but are

The Move and Accommodation

expensive on the pocket and the clothes, possibly because of the strength of washing detergent used and the way shirts are machine ironed which tends to split the buttons. Use as little washing fluid or powder as possible, and cut out ironing and, speaking as a man, clothes last longer and seem clean enough.

Dry cleaning is another story. I find it cannot be avoided and again saves the ironing of trousers. It is estimated that the average German housewife spends 40 DM on washing, cleaning etc, but only a few marks monthly on dry cleaning.

Insurance

If your household effects are still insured with a home insurance company, it may be very expensive to continue insuring them abroad. It might be much cheaper to change to a local company. Like everything else insurance is a subject on which you should take advice. The main points to be taken into consideration are:
1. Make a list of all effects with a valuation of all valuables which must be quoted in the contract (keep the valuation up to date). A German insurance company will not reimburse fully for separate items of high value unless declared as such in the contract.
2. In case of burglary, but where there is no sign or proof of entry (smashed lock, door or window), nothing will be paid. It could be an inside job — see next section.

Security

German door locks usually work on the self-closing system, that is they lock automatically when you close the door. You cannot put a lock on the latch. This is excellent for security because it means that the lock is never dead, but it can mean that it is easy to lock yourself out.

Some locks are lockable from inside with the key in the lock but then can be opened from outside too (even if the key is still in the lock inside). Others preclude this happening. If you are in a hurry it is easy to forget that the key is in the lock inside (*Schlüssel steckt*), go out, pull the door to and then find that you are locked out. It is then necessary to fetch a locksmith which is extremely expensive. The best thing is to use only one key and never to leave the flat without it. Any other key (spare key) should be kept elsewhere. Never use two keys for the same

The Move and Accommodation

lock. If you do, you will be tempted to leave the key inside the door and then shut yourself out.

When you go on holiday, you will need to stop the newspaper delivery but milk is not delivered as in England. You will find, though, that the Federal Post has a very efficient system of forwarding mail (*Nachsendungseantrag*) which is free (*kostenlos*).

Getting things repaired

Finding someone to repair a gadget, watch or clock is an art as with any country. It may be more difficult for a foreigner because the item concerned is not a local product. Spare parts may not be available and the craftsman may be unfamiliar with the make. It pays to enquire first, especially with watches. There are some butchers about and they can wreak havoc with an old watch. There are also some excellent craftsmen who appreciate old things and take a joy and pride in repairing them. I have found that the most voluble craftsmen are the worst and the more reticent ones the best. The same holds for car mechanics. Garages used to be dreadful, especially those repairing British cars. The main problem was that they were not properly supervised by the manufacturers and, because initial quality of production was poor, they found themselves in the unenviable position of having — or so they felt — to virtually rebuild the whole car for which the amount of reimbursement under the guarantee was barely, if at all, sufficient. Apparently things are improving on this score which, if true, is indeed welcome news.

Garages

When renting accommodation always enquire about the availability of a garage. Not all flats include a garage or use of space in the underground car park. You may well find it advisable not to park your car on the street overnight. It could be broken open and it is a fearful business scraping the ice off the windscreen and, sometimes, even starting the engine on winter mornings. If garage space is not available, you may be able to rent space either on a park deck or in a lot in front of the block of flats.

Housework: cleaning

Housework can be kept to a minimum by using to the full the gadgets available. Fitted carpets help. Most German housewives

The Move and Accommodation

use vacuum cleaners as opposed to the Hoover (*Klopfsauger*) type of carpet cleaner which 'beats as it cleans'. In the courtyard of blocks of flats special bars are always available on which tenants can beat their rugs.

Window cleaning is a personal responsibility for each flat dweller. Window cleaners service office blocks but seldom blocks of flats. Be careful not to fall out! The earlier German double-glazed windows required cleaning on the inside of each pane, which was most time-consuming, but with the modern type window this is, mercifully, no longer necessary.

What is a trial of patience and manual dexterity as well as testing to your back is taking down inner curtains (*Stores*), washing them, and them putting them back on the runner attached to the ceiling. The little hooks are easy enough to fit into the runner but the tricky, fiddly, backbreaking part comes when you have to fit the plastic stopper between the penultimate and the last hook. As the *Stores* are wet and heavy — it's unnecessary to iron or fully dry them before replacement — you are battling against the forces of gravity as well as trying to keep your balance (you need the dexterity of a serpent again). This is a moment in every long stayer's life when he or she wonders whether everything is worthwhile!

Some locals go overboard and become what Germans call a *Putzteufel*, a cleaning maniac. I have a friend, a senior local government official, who devotes part of his annual holiday to cleaning out his flat. He will even devote the odd Sunday as well to doing it.

There are many *Putzteufel* in Germany, especially car owners who devote — or so it seems — every available moment to polishing their cars. One wonders whether they ever get round to driving their immaculate machines.

Noise

One of the joys of living in Germany if you are a sensitive soul about noise, is that there are strict regulations to curb noise levels in blocks of flats and in the garden. One of the 'curses' for the hobby enthusiast who is never happier than when doing household repairs or mowing the lawn, is that he may easily fall foul of a neighbour who is sensitive about noise.

You may take it as a rule of thumb that noise is not permitted

59

The Move and Accommodation

(except on building sites where work usually starts at 6 am!) between the following times (*Ruhezeiten*):
Monday – Friday: before 08.00
                12 to 14.00
                after 20.00
Saturday: before 08.00 and from 12.00 onwards.
Sunday and public holidays: all day.

It is as well to observe these regulations if you want to keep the peace and avoid either solicitor's letters or the threat of court proceedings from the local municipal authority (*Ordnungsamt*). Aggrieved citizens will not hesitate to call the police to enforce local anti-noise regulations.

Telephone bills

Telephone bills are sent monthly; the best way to pay is by debit transfer (*Lastschriftverfahren*), whereby the amount is simply debited against your bank account. Otherwise if you forget to pay, the line will be disconnected, etc.

The bill will show the number of units (at 23 Pfg) that have been used, contains a monthly regular charge (*Gebühr*) and gives any extras, such as operator or connected calls, telegrams, early morning calls (*Weckdienst*), etc.

City services: garbage collection

City services usually include garbage disposal by specially operated trucks that take only a certain type of dustbin, which house owners, or the administrators of blocks of flats, must buy. The charge for rubbish collection is usually included in the *Nebenkosten* (additional costs) contract and seems to be increased regularly. So-called *Sperrmüll* (that is, large, unwieldy items of furniture) are collected on special days from each district. You can obtain a timetable for such collections from the town hall.

Germans have become very environmentally conscious, some flat administrators more than others, so sometimes special containers are provided for glass. Elsewhere, large containers are placed near shopping centres so that people can dispose of their bottles whilst shopping.

General municipal garbage disposal has become a serious problem in West Germany and determined efforts are being

The Move and Accommodation

made to encourage stores and supermarkets to use only biodegradable plastic bags.

Gas and electricity
The city services also provide electricity and gas and, for some large office and apartment blocks, district heating (*Fernheizung*). The main concern of the customer is the cost. Electricity and gas meters are read at the end of each year or bi-monthly. The most convenient way to pay is to have the amount debited accordingly against your bank account (*Lastschriftverfahren*).
When you move in or out it is obviously essential to have the meter read. The same holds for the meters that measure the amount of heating used on the radiators in flats (see *Heating*).

The bill
With the price of oil varying and the price of gas (ie, coal) remaining fairly constant because it is heavily subsidised, the unit for oil district heating (*Fernheizung*) is fixed in relation to the price of gas in order that everyone should be treated equally should there be an undue difference in the material cost of either source of energy.

7
Being Moneywise

Money

For the long stayer it is as well to understand right from the start the German attitude to money. It is very businesslike and some visitors might find such an attitude very hard. There are certain basic rules: never buy or pay for anything until you are sure that you want it. Don't expect to get your money back, even if you think you should. Ultimately, if it comes to a disagreement it is the judge in court who will have to decide. You will save yourself a lot of disappointment, time and energy by not rushing in to buy, hire or rent anything. Never sign on the dotted line of any agreement or contract without first reading every word, and if you do not understand the document, ask someone who does to explain it to you (see *Rented accommodation*). If you follow this advice, you will most probably save yourself many times the price of this volume. Prevention is better than cure! It is invidious here to generalise, but it is well worth noting that Germans are excellent salesmen but tend to be much less sympathetic if you want your money back. Be very, very careful! Germans themselves are very careful and ask many questions before they sign documents and buy things.

You must take into account the economic history of Germany; there have been two economic crises – the greatest inflation was from 1921 to 1923 after World War I, and the *Währungsreform* (currency reform) in 1948 after World War II. Having seen their money become virtually worthless twice within a lifetime, makes people suspicious and very careful with it. One does not extend credit until a customer is known, be it at a garage or in a shop (however there are credit cards galore, but less so than in the States).

Using German banks

A good banking connection makes life easier anywhere, especially for a foreigner residing in Germany. An efficient bank

Being Moneywise

can settle by bankers orders monthly or bi-monthly bills, annual subscriptions and obligations which, if not paid promptly, could lead to unpleasant consequences, not the least being an inordinate waste of time and energy. Germans expect bills to be paid punctually and where this does not occur and reminders are ignored, the *Gerichtsvollzieher* (bailiff) swings into action with power to impound the debtor's effects. If the *Gerichtsvollzieher* cannot gain entry, in your absence, then he is not above making enquiries about his client's creditworthiness among the neighbours, which can be *most* embarrassing. It is therefore advisable to pay bills promptly, best of all automatically, which is possible with an efficient bank. How do you find one?

Basically German banks, be they saving banks (*Sparkassen*) or ordinary banks, private (*Privatbanken*) or commercial joint-stock taking banks (*Aktienbanken*), are all the same in dealing with their customers because they use the same system, laid down by law (the *Kreditwesengesetz* — KWG for short) and because they share the same structure.

The bank manager as the British see him — a father-confessor to whom one goes to beg for overdrafts — just does not exist in Germany. The average customer deals mostly with individual departments within the branch, assuming it is of a reasonable size. The branch manager (*Direktor*, as he is called), concerns himself mainly with more affluent private customers or firms. There may well be two co-managers, rather than a manager and his deputy, and both may sign the same letters.

They, and the whole bank, work according to a system. The essence of this is that the customer is informed of every single movement (*Kontobewegung*) or transaction on a *Kontoauszug* (account slip), which is mailed on the same or next day, or made available to the customer for collection. If there are several transactions in a day, they will be recorded on the one *Kontoauszug*. Thus the customer keeps abreast of the balance of his account more easily than under the British and American systems with their monthly or even quarterly statements. It is essential, given this system, to keep the relevant slips of paper in the folder provided. If you do not do this fairly methodically, you can soon lose track of the payments into and out of your account. If required, most banks will supply a print-out statement similar to that provided by

63

Being Moneywise

British banks, but most local customers do not require this service.

Old encashed cheques are kept by the bank, but Xeroxed copies can be obtained.

German banks give attractive freebies to customers; diaries and maps, as well as folders to keep the account slips (*Kontoauszüge*) in order, which are well worth using.

Opening hours are usually from 8 to 12.15 and from 14.00 to 16.00 Monday through to Friday, except Thursday with late closing at 17.30. Few banks open on Saturday mornings. Many banks have automatic cash dispensers but few will accept and register deposits, though of course there are the usual business facilities for receiving cash containers.

Changing money

Of extreme importance is the foreign department (*Auslandsabteilung*) of your local bank, responsible for foreign exchange. Unlike US banks, customers are quoted the daily rate of exchange for cheques and not an international bank rate, which is much lower than the former. A charge of 1.5 per cent (per thousand) is made on each transaction, be it a cheque or draft. The minimum charge is DM 15 (approx £5). A friendly bank clerk will allow you the best rate of exchange between the day before and the day in question. It won't make much difference but a few extra marks are always welcome.

There is an art in having money transferred to Germany. The simplest method is a draft. Whoever sends the money from abroad buys a draft in DM at home and sends it by post to your bank which then credits it minus a small fee (*Gebühr*) to your account. The home bank can be entrusted to do this, but in my experience banks rarely do it quickly. The transaction has to go through too many channels and takes an inordinate amount of time.

A traveller's cheque in DM is another method, with 'For the account of (your name)' entered on the requisite line. The cheque should be dated and signed back and front by the sender and marked '& Co' on the front, like a normal crossed cheque, so that the cheque is valueless to the thief, if stolen. If you have no account, cheques should not be crossed, but sent by registered post, though there is still an element of risk involved.

Being Moneywise

Eurocheques, backed by a Eurocheque card (which in some countries can be used with a pin number to obtain money out of a dispenser), are useful, but enquire at your home bank what the additional charges are likely to be. I have always found the best and cheapest way of transferring money from home is to have my own British cheques credited to my local German account.

Small change

One additional, indirect, source of money is to let the cashier of the bank know you collect small change in your own currency. Tourists often bring small change to Germany and seek to convert it into marks for which they get a very poor rate of exchange. The bank is usually delighted to get rid of such money at a very favourable rate of exchange for the buyer. If you do not mind the inconvenience of carrying home to the UK a small bag of coins, you will find the money has its full value there.

There are many ways of saving money and few students can afford to ignore them.

Bank charges

A recent court judgement laid down that banks are no longer allowed to postpone crediting customers' (*Wertstellung*) deposits whilst immediately debiting withdrawals. The effect of this enabled banks to save or make money on the time between receipt of a customer's cheque and crediting the amount to the relevant account. This problem was particularly acute over weekends, public holidays, especially over Christmas and the New Year when several days could elapse before the transaction was recorded.

Banks now complain that the whole procedure of managing private customers' accounts (as opposed to business ones) has become too costly — the *Dresdner Bank* claimed that the previous system was worth DM 20 million to them. Now that such savings are forbidden them, the *Dresdner Bank* has decided to charge customers 60 Pfennig which they claim is only 29.4 per cent of the actual cost, some 3.45 DM for each entry. I think that German banks could be far more cost effective if they were not required (or simply refused) to issue a *Kontoauszug* for each transaction and if they simply introduced detailed monthly or yearly statements instead like Coutts Bank in England. The only problem with such an arrangement would be the impossibility of businesses having an up-to-date check on the state of their accounts.

Credit for cars
Long stayers might find it difficult at the start of their stay to obtain credit, such as a bank loan, to buy a car locally. It makes sense to open an account with a local bank immediately upon arrival so that a relationship of mutual trust can be built up. The bank will worry about long term repayment of a loan in the case of those on short term contracts.

Buying a house
To own a house, one's own four walls, may be the aim of almost every German, but would it make sense for a temporary or even for a long term visitor?

This is a much easier question to answer for the temporary visitor; 'No', unless you have a lot of spare cash and wish to speculate against the value of the property going up in a relatively short time (which might well happen in a very popular area such as Munich) of if it is a flat or a house in the country to which you could return for holidays or let to others, thus ensuring a regular income in German marks (though there might be local tax liability, depending upon the amount involved). But this would be high-flying for most.

The long term visitor might also find property a good investment but conventional wisdom is that it is cheaper to rent accommodation. If you are dependent upon obtaining the highest rate of interest for capital available, then capital invested in the market will bring a higher rate of return than by investing it in property.

However, property can sometimes be purchased relatively cheaply or under the market price at *Zwangsversteigerungen*, forced sales of bankrupt owners. Information can be obtained from the local courts (*Amtsgerichte*).

Buying property
British readers will rejoice that there is no 'gazumping' in Germany. Everything is managed contractually.

Raising the money

Assuming that you have no private funds and no subsidy or grant from your employer, then finance is a personal matter and of course vital. It is probably the most important investment you will make in Germany and requires considerable thought. The sum required to buy or build a house probably represents at least twenty years' salary and may well take up to thirty years to pay back. Any wrong decision taken now could prejudice your future financial position despite the fact that property values have risen hitherto, though the extent to which they rise depends on the district.

Like most things in Germany it requires specialised knowledge to obtain a loan from a bank or building society *(Bausparkasse)*. Consider this example: you want to *buy* a house costing DM 300,000 (approximately £100,000). If you have the cash, then you need not raise the money by taking out a loan, but you should consider whether the capital you possess, be it already invested in stocks or shares or in a high interest yield account, is not more profitably invested where it is, rather than in a house which (depending upon its situation) might or might not appreciate in value. You are a long stayer, but there again you might have to leave early and then have the problem of selling or letting the house quickly. Selling quickly often means being forced to accept a lower price than necessary and consequent loss of capital. Letting property quickly in a foreign country might prove unsatisfactory too, although a good estate agent should be able to arrange things, but then finding a competent estate agent in a hurry might also prove difficult.

If you decide to buy, as opposed to building a house (which obviously takes time while you must find somewhere else to live), then you have to borrow money from a bank or from a building society; the advantage of the former is that you can obtain the loan on a mortgage at the normal rate (7 to 10 per cent depending upon the length of the loan); the advantage of the latter is that you can take out two mortgages and more cheaply.

Savings agreement with a building society
(Bausparvertrag)
Would-be borrowers pay 20–50 per cent of the sum they require into a building society account over several years

(*Bausparvertrag*). Interest is paid by the building society on this sum. After say, two to three years, the society, which then has sufficient money at its disposal to finance a certain number of houses, chooses a few members, who receive loans at a low rate of interest, to begin a mortgage. The selection procedure is determined according to a formula that takes into account the value of the mortgage, how long it took to pay in the 50 per cent and the average yearly payments. However long you must wait for the loan, usually in the long run it is cheaper to wait than to borrow the money from a bank.

It is important to remember that the security on the loan is always the house itself, so that if you default on the loan repayments you forfeit the house, although you can insure yourself to some extent against your dependants losing the house if the default is through death, accident or illness. Moreover you can take out insurance before repayments (*Tilgungen*) begin. Of course you have to pay the insurance premiums but these total less than the sum mortgaged and thus combined with bonus payments should cover the whole mortgage sum.

A building society (*Bausparkasse*) will provide the money more cheaply than a bank, but will usually only lend the final sum to start building when half of the necessary money has been paid into the customer's account with the society. If the sum required is DM 300,000 and half (DM 150,000) is needed to obtain the whole loan, assuming you have already paid in DM 75,000, a temporary loan of DM 75,000 (*Zwischenfinanzierung*) could be borrowed from a bank to fill the gap. Of course, the temporary loan will attract a higher rate of interest, but once the DM 300,000 have been advanced by the building society the DM 75,000 can be repaid to the bank immediately and the interest correspondingly reduced.

There are of course other means of financing the purchase of a house, geared to different individual circumstances. Younger people usually want longer to pay off the debt, while older ones can better afford to clear it quickly.

Tax consideration
One advantage of building, as opposed to buying, a house is that certain tax reductions are granted according to the size of the loan required for building or, with a *Bausparvertrag*, in

relation to the yearly amount saved in advance to obtain the loan. Moreover the value of the house is given at 50 per cent of its market value — the *Einheitswert* — for the purpose of computing the wealth tax (*Vermögenssteuer*).

Notary
The contract to buy a house has to be examined by a *Notar* (notary) who advises both parties to the contract on their rights and obligations in the matter.

Land register
When buying a house or plot (*Grundstück*) on which to build a house, it is essential to examine the land register (*Grundbuch*) to ensure that a) the seller is the true owner and b) that there is no mortgage or sequestration. If the seller is the true owner and it is free of any obligations, you must ensure that the house or land when purchased is entered in your name. Entry in the *Grundbuch* is proof of ownership.

Having invested so much money in a house it is as well to consider the general economic state of the country in which you have invested.

Economics (buying power)
Precisely because Germans have suffered two periods of enormous inflation in this century most people expect the government above all else to keep inflation under control. Whilst the cost of living rose by an average of 6 per cent per annum since the 1970s, in December 1986 the cost of living fell for the first time in almost thirty years. This was mainly because of a sharp fall in the price of oil. The government is careful not to distort market forces by interventionist measures except in transport and agriculture. The main problem West Germany has to face is shortage of raw materials which are mainly imported, although there are modest deposits of iron ore and petroleum in the country, as well as brown coal and hard coal for which demand has been falling in favour of oil, gas and nuclear power. And it is there that political problems arise; the environmentalists, in particular the Greens, are opposed to nuclear power — especially in Brokdorf — and saw their fears realised by Chernobyl.

As far as balancing the budget is concerned, the export trade — especially with America — is of prime importance but declined recently because of the weak dollar and the strong mark. West Germany is able to iron out certain difficulties even in that market because 'Made in Germany' is still very much a sign of quality. As a founder member and as a pillar of the Common Market, Germany has been able to find a second base for her export trade.

8
Business Relationships

We now move from the material to the socio–spiritual, from worrying about money, cars and houses to getting on with people.

Taking German life seriously
You may find on arrival the cultural shock so great and the bureaucratic requirements so demanding, that everything takes your breath away. Remember that essentially it is all a game, even if it appears to be a serious one. The rules and regulations cover everything and I would do you a disservice if I suggested that they should be disregarded. However, there are usually ways round most regulations and some laws. It is a matter of juggling one regulation against another; there are so many of them and nearly as many exceptions, so you have a good chance of finding a legitimate way round a particular problem. This approach does not always work but it certainly does some of the time. Things are not as strict as they seem.

Self-criticism: going in for extremes
Germans are at times very self-critical. They often acknowledge that they tend to opt for 'extremes' — they do nothing by halves. One notices it in different aspects of daily life: the early morning start, eg the chimney sweep (*Kaminkehrer*) who comes at 6 am to check your heater; and the extent to which bureaucracy borders on the absurd. It does have its good side, eg the little rail and peg at the back of the cheapest German car or above third class seats on trains for hanging your coats; little gadgets for some simple but otherwise fiddly things. In general, meticulous thought and planning goes into the simplest things, so often maddeningly absent in products of English-speaking nations.

German thought processes
Germans think completely differently from English-speaking people. They have a high respect for and trust in the written

word, in the 'system' as such. One reason for Britain entering World War I was that Germany attacked France through Belgium, the neutrality of which had been guaranteed years before by England. The Germans insisted on going through Belgium in accordance with the von Schlieffen Plan, although von Schlieffen was already dead when war broke out. Failing a system, nothing gets done. You are lost — or put another way, there is no premium on flexibility. Of course, there are ways round the system but you will put people's backs up if you make a point of not observing it. I remember visiting a museum on a Sunday. It was empty except for the attendant. He got furious when I went round the exhibits in the opposite direction to which the arrows pointed (the *Führungslinie*). As I was the only visitor at the time and he the only attendant it did not seem to matter but he became apoplectic! I suppose in his many years of service no-one had ever before refused to follow the *Führungslinie*.

Now I have learnt not to kick up a fuss and just follow the *Führungslinie*. I remember complaining about the late postal delivery to my block of flats — 1.30 pm. I saw the local postmaster about it. 'Oh', he said, 'my post comes late too.' He then added in explanation: 'You see, it's the system' (*Das System*). It didn't occur to him that his system was obviously not working and needed changing. These are, apart from the von Schlieffen Plan, not profound but everyday examples of a state of mind. And you should be aware of it.

The problem of integration — no social hang-ups

How long will it take to integrate into the German way of life? Some long stayers never manage it nor do they really try; others succeed due only to local kindness and understanding.

Germany has no class system as such, virtually no private education, gentlemen's clubs and social appurtenances that debar the non-initiated from joining in. German aristocracy is small and of little significance. There is no upper-middle class, in the English sense. There are rich, fairly prosperous, prosperous and middle and lower income groups. You can tell them by the size of their houses and cars and not by accent, education and other social imponderables.

It is thus a very open society. The distinctions are purely

Business Relationships

according to income and then to region. Germany, for historical reasons, has always been regional. Unity first occurred in 1871, imposed by Bismarck, with the creation of the German Empire which was proclaimed at the end of the Franco-Prussian War in Versailles. The November Revolution in 1918 put an end to that. The Weimar Republic collapsed and Adolf Hitler took over to introduce his 1,000 Year *Reich* which lasted only twelve years, collapsing in 1945.

Germany still is, in many respects, merely a collection of regions (the *Länder*) joined together in a federal state. Germans' loyalty is usually first to the region. They think of themselves as Berliners, Swabians or Bavarians and only secondly as Germans with a big G.

You are not likely to become integrated into German regional life if you are permanently based in an international city, such as Frankfurt or a cosmopolitan one as Bonn. However, if you have a family you will probably live out in the country, and there you will soon become aware of regional traditions and loyalties.

The interesting thing for a foreigner about such regional associations is that they often reflect foreign connections. Again, this can be understood through Germany's history. Many German mercenaries served in the American War of Independence in the eighteenth century and settled down there afterwards, and then later on even more Germans emigrated to the States. Following the War of Independence it was only decided by a one-vote majority against making German the official language. At the time of World War I, more than 8 per cent of Americans were of German extraction.

Bavaria has many connections with France, Scotland and England as well as America. The *Englischer Garten* (English Park) of the American Loyalist, Benjamin Thompson (later Lord Rumford) in Munich bears witness to this triangular US–UK–Bavarian connection. He was a celebrated local social reformer and later founded the Royal Institution in London. It is this German regional internationalism which explains the existence of such a surprising number of excellent German provincial art collections, such as the *Alte Pinakothek* in Munich and, of course, which makes Germany such a culturally rewarding and pleasant place to live in, even in the provinces.

Business Relationships

Hierarchic thinking

When working in a large German organisation it is as well to realise that people think very hierarchically. Everybody is treated with respect. Seldom (except at manual worker level) are first names used between colleagues. Everyone, including the doorman or porter, is addressed as *'Herr'*, *'Frau'* or *'Fräulein'*. Exceptions exist among foreign workers or colleagues and at university students address each other with the familiar *'Du'*; also in sport (ski-ing, volley ball etc). No-one calls the boss by his first name as in some English-speaking countries (nor do secretaries call executives by theirs). My students who take internships with British companies say that the boss–employee relationship is far more subtle in England than in Germany. Certainly in my experience the boss — *der Chef* or *Abteilungsleiter* — is very much more the boss and is anxious that this should not be forgotten. To point this out is not to be critical.

The system, especially the formality, has its advantages. An employee is not seduced into confusing his job with his personal life. The division between work and home is most pronounced in Germany. It is part and parcel of the *Beamtenstaat* philosophy (see *Beamtenstaat – officialdom*) and is reflected in the language (see *Language*), especially the difference between the formal 'You' (*Sie*) and the informal, familiar 'You' (*Du*) ie 'thou'. You must get used to it and not have false expectations of enjoying the same degree of informal conviviality that may exist in English-speaking organisations.

Finally it must be repeated that Germany unlike England does not have a class system. Germany does not have an upper-middle class educated at exclusive schools and universities, no equivalent of Sloane Rangers or the old-school tie. Hence there are no social bridges at work cutting across hierarchical boundaries as in England or America. There are Rotary and Lions and of course the *Verbindungen* (male associations formed at university and membership of political parties — see *Verbindungen* and *political parties*) but nothing to compare with English-speaking social relationships based on a different history and social culture.

There are, of course, sports clubs (athletics, badminton, tennis, ski, soccer etc) but nothing to compare with English-speaking club life and the social implications that go with it. Obviously business colleagues do go out for a drink together and there are

Betriebsausflüge (outings); an employer (shopkeeper or the like) will take out his employees for a meal at Christmas, but there the matter ends.

People tend to be divided between the formal *Sie* and the informal family, free-time *Du*. You may take a while to get used to the differentiation, but eventually you will. This does not mean to say that there are no exceptions. You may become friendly with a colleague or fellow employee at the office and he or she might well invite you home to meet the family, especially because you are a foreigner. But don't except it or be disappointed if it doesn't occur. And as a corollary you should think very carefully before trying to take the initiative. Unless you develop a true friendship all the hospitality and resulting relationship will be just a ritual. People are expected to know their place and to respect each other's privacy. It may seem cool, and excessively formal but the system has its advantages. There is no danger of 'familiarity breeding contempt'. There is no enforced mateyness that can be so trying if you have difficulty with a boss or colleague. The German way of doing things has to be understood before it can be judged, observed or disregarded.

Beware of first names: familiarity breeds contempt
It pays to be wary of trying out *Du* and first names on colleagues as a foreigner; wait and see how they behave in this respect. If everyone is on first name terms, fine, unless you are senior to them. Whereas in English-speaking countries the custom is that even if first names are used, the boss is still recognised and treated as the boss, German colleagues might find this difficult to accept. Far better to seek advice from an older colleague. At university, in my experience even with English-speaking colleagues, it is better to be wary of using first names because it may well be taken as a licence to familiarity. There will be occasions when you will be grateful to be able to keep some colleagues at arms' length with a certain amount of formality. It is easier to unbend than to tighten up. In any case the whole situation is complicated by the fact that you are in a *German* place of work.

Students may prefer to be called by their first names and addressed as *Du* by teachers of their own age —

remember that German students are usually much older than their English-speaking equivalents. In my experience though, treating students as equals confuses them and can well lead to difficulties at exam time when a student who has been addressed as *Du* and reciprocated with his teacher imagines that the cosy, familiar relationship entitles him or her to a good mark regardless of performance. This leads to difficulties for those colleagues who are not on *Du* terms with students. The best advice ever given to me was to save the *Du*-relationship to after the exams thus avoiding all misunderstanding. I have always followed it and found that it worked every time. However, this does not prevent a teacher treating mature and trustworthy students in a more informal yet nonetheless mutually respectful way.

Egalitarianism
A formal working atmosphere should not belie the egalitarian approach to industrial relations, which is part and parcel of the German work ethic. There are no rigid visible divisions between white and blue collar workers in large concerns. Everyone eats in the same canteen — no special managers' dining room; the same at universities where senior common rooms or faculty clubs do not exist. Everyone mucks in together, which is excellent in one way because it removes possible grounds for complaint on the part of the blue collar workers, but it also no doubt encourages senior management to eat at home and thus prevents them communicating with each other during the 30-minute lunch breaks. Those who eat sandwiches at their desks, communicating with colleagues only in writing, would often find a quick word over after-lunch coffee more efficient. It is a *Beamtenstaat* in miniature. Things must be done the official way and if they are not, then they tend not to get done, which can be very frustrating for those who think and work creatively. There is a premium on conformity.

Egalitarianism is also exemplified in the works' councils which are legally and constitutionally part of every company, above a certain size, and are intended to guarantee the rights of employees. Undoubtedly their welfare function is very useful for the employees, but they do not necessarily make for the efficient running of an organisation. This brings in politics,

Business Relationships

which is outside the scope of this book. The important thing is that such organisations exist in German industry and have to be taken seriously or certainly into account. Dissatisfied works' councils have the right of appeal to the labour courts, which can be a time-consuming process for all. It pays management to tread very carefully when dealing with workers' complaints and to realise, when starting up in Germany, the inhibiting effect that workers' councils can have on productivity and efficiency.

Smoking
As in the States, protection is guaranteed for non-smokers, that is, those who become 'passive smokers' when others are smoking. Non-smokers may object in an office if a colleague smokes and the law obliges the colleague to desist.

The Betriebsausflug (annual outing)
An example of the German attempt to conduct industrial relations amicably is the *Betriebsausflug* which is an annual excursion arranged for everyone in a company or institution. The idea is that everyone should get to know each other in a relaxed atmosphere. In fact mainly only manual workers and secretaries tend to go with only some of the senior staff joining in out of a sense of duty. Some employees prefer to stay at their desks rather than spend a day off in this way. Nevertheless for some companies and institutions the *Betriebsausflug* works very well.

Doing business with Germans
It helps if you know the language or make an effort to speak a few words. Germans are very polite and helpful in this respect. In any case they can usually speak English. However, I have often heard that they are amazed how the majority of British salesmen presume to sell their products in their own language and make little effort to make allowances for the fact that the customer speaks and reads another language. Sales literature in English without a translation is surely a poor way to sell a product, especially if it is a technical one.

Moreover, it is customary for the seller to invite the customer to lunch and not the other way round. Germans sometimes get

Business Relationships

the impression that British salesmen take insufficient trouble to become conversant with local business etiquette. On the other hand German salesmen are usually punctilious in this respect in English-speaking countries. It seems a pity not to reciprocate.

English-speaking companies could certainly make it a lot easier for their employees working abroad if they would arrange language and customs courses before sending their people overseas.

German business people are usually very busy and life is hectic but they do appreciate at least some ritual, be it in making the gesture of speaking their language, in being interested in the country or in observing the courtesies of entertainment. All this will assuredly pay tremendous dividends, not only in obtaining orders but also in patience if delivery dates are postponed or if the quality is, for some reason, not up to standard — although these two key elements, if repeated, are a recipe for disaster.

Germans tend to be more commercially minded than their British counterparts. They understand to a certain point that a relaxed attitude to work represents greater importance attached to human values — they (the Germans) respect this, but they prefer to concentrate on the business in hand. Business comes first; if that is all right, then fine, but if not, there is no mercy. They can always buy elsewhere. Theirs is a completely different attitude to work and profit. They don't have any social hang-ups about making profits nor about working hard, even competing ruthlessly, to get those profits. This, in turn, reflects a harder, more realistic attitude to life.

Morals

The German moral code is based on compromise. It is not absolute. There is an official — according to the book with all its exceptions — and a private morality. This is said to provide a framework for understanding certain essentially un-British habits. Germans have an expression *'Kavaliersdelikt'* (a peccadillo), that is, general approval to do certain things (if you can get away with it) which would be unacceptable in English-speaking countries.

Students are not above cheating in tests and exams and

feel no shame in so doing — see *Exams*. Law students are sometimes the worst. I have heard that they even steal each other's books before the exam in the examination hall. Older, more knowledgeable, students will write tests for their junior less well-versed colleagues. The other students don't mind and members of staff do not seem to be very concerned. If a student is caught then appropriate action will be taken; but they seldom are. All sorts of subterfuges are resorted to: crib notes hidden up sleeves, even longer crib notes to be referred to in the loo and in real doubt, other methods too. The same happens at school.

The same ambivalent attitude to cheating holds with telling the truth. In Germany it is a rather relative concept. It is not absolute and sacred. The German word *lügen* (to lie) has both a serious and less serious shade of meaning. Whilst in English you would never as a joke accuse someone of lying, in Germany you can. You often hear two people teasing each other. The one tells the other something and the other says jokingly '*Du lügst*'; it is not meant as an insult.

The relative attitude to truth is not because Germans are necessarily less honest than English-speaking people. It is because a German never wants to offend you. One is seldom told 'No' or simply refused something. One is told 'Nein, das geht schlecht' (No, that is difficult) or 'Na, ja', (Well, perhaps). There is significantly always that wonderful word 'Njein' which is a mixture of 'Ja' (yes) and 'Nein' (no) and usually means 'No' but a 'no' that under certain conditions can become a 'Yes'.

The whole business of answering questions or stating an opinion is far more subtle in German. It must not be forgotten that during the Third Reich people were stuck in concentration camps, tortured and gassed for speaking their minds and there are still people alive who remember it.

The corollary of this is that Germans do not appreciate bluntness. They regard it as rude and unfeeling or as they would say 'plump' (tactless). In England bluntness is accepted as a virtue, as a sign of honesty, not so in Germany. The best thing, if you are not sure of how to deal with a particular person or situation, is to take one's cue from the German with whom you are negotiating. If you do this, you will probably come to a better understanding than by behaving as you would at home.

Business Relationships

Trust
You trust friends and colleagues if you know them. In general be careful. Do not believe what people say until they can prove it. You may believe it, but do not act on it. This means that people are expected to produce identity cards and certificates and enormous importance is attached to pieces of paper, rubber stamps and signatures.

'Ja, ich glaube schon, aber Sie müssen mir Ihren Ausweis (Schein usw) zeigen.'

'Yes, I believe you, really I do, but I still have to see your identity card (certificate, etc).'

I have heard this many times. And it is no good kicking against the pricks!

This does not mean to say that Germans, especially officials, cannot be extremely understanding to foreigners. But don't rely upon this happening. It is not a right. And if it happens, once, twice or thrice don't assume that it will always occur. He or she is only doing you a favour and may well resent having to do it.

Dress
Degree in formality of dress varies enormously depending upon the occasion and the person. Generally people dress to please themselves. Young people wear jeans as if they had to; they (the jeans) have almost become *de rigueur*. The same holds for many adults, but at work men wear slacks and trousers, shirt and often no tie while women often wear trousers. Bank clerks, though not always, tend to wear suits, as do senior officials, commercial travellers and businessmen. Most German men have a blue suit, usually dark, which is worn for best occasions. There appears to be little distinction between, as in England, town and country suits; brown is considered to be unbecoming; country tweeds for men seem to be unknown; trousers always seem to be pressed. The rather sloppy-looking, upper-class or Sloane Ranger country attire is largely unknown. A German has to try hard to look untidy, unless he is a tramp. There is no equivalent of the scruffy-looking British aristocrat.

Germans claim that British trousers are old-fashioned and the bespoke ones look as though they were tailored at the turn of the century. I found the best compromise was to have a jacket and waistcoat made in England and the trousers in Germany.

Business Relationships

German jackets do not look as though they were tailored in Savile Row and (though this is a personal opinion) are generally without distinction, rather they may have been made for waiters or bouncers! Women dress informally. Fashions are mainly copied from abroad and clothes come off the peg. Many women, especially in country districts, still have dressmakers but this is on grounds of economy rather than aiming for distinctive fashion. German female beauty is based on curvacious healthy bodies, often blooming, sometimes buxom, but rarely graceful or refined. At least that is my general impression; German women are superb creatures in every way but, like the menfolk, they usually lack sophistication unless they have been abroad and become cosmopolitan.

In country districts women may wear regional costumes (*Tracht*) or country peasant dress as of yore. Germany is still very much a rural country, although only a minority of the population is engaged in agriculture. However those that are, look the part in a picturesque way.

German cleanliness
Germany is a remarkably clean country compared to others. Cleanliness is an extension of the German penchant for having things just right. One is grateful for it. Lavatories are usually clean, public buildings properly swept. Trains and buses are clean too. Order enters into everything. It is a country of locks and keys; everything is locked up and woe betide whoever loses a key.

Everything is neat and tidy. There is a saying: 'Ordnung muß sein'. After a time you become used to and indeed grateful for it. Everything has its place, there is a law or regulation governing, so it seems, every aspect of human life literally from the cradle to the grave. To a foreigner this can seem absurd. You can either kick against the pricks and remain as you are, or you can comply. You must decide if you want to become integrated into the German way of life; paperwork, residence permits, etc, have already been discussed, and you can save considerable time and frustration by getting them right. What is slightly more difficult is deciding on an appropriate lifestyle. Whereas in England it is acceptable to wear scruffy, uncreased

Business Relationships

trousers unless on business, in Germany it is not. They have a word '*schmuddelig*' for someone whose appearance does not come up to scratch; a Britisher's often does not.

You can do what you like but after spending several years in the country (and this would apply to some long stayers) it is difficult not to become aware of the mild disdain that greets a scruffy appearance. No-one will say anything, but will think plenty. This also applies to personal hygiene.

German standards are high. Rarely do you see Germans scratching themselves. They have a saying: 'Nicht kratzen, sondern waschen!' ('Don't scratch, wash!'). People wash, shower or bath as well as cleaning their teeth before going to bed; and are most particular about doing so. However you do see people relieving themselves or allowing their children to relieve themselves in the street! And no-one seems aware that a contradiction is involved. The same goes for spitting in the gutter. I lived for eight years in Munich and noticed the abandon with which people did this. I can only conclude that the physical need to do so is caused by central heating, which makes the respiratory system produce an excess of mucous and phlegm.

Always wipe your shoes on the doormat before entering someone's home. You will be told not to bother, but it will be appreciated. Sometimes you will be offered special slippers or house shoes if you take your shoes off, but this is only usual when you know the person or family well.

Cleanliness is at a premium. Every office seems to have a wash basin. Germans wear overalls or an apron to keep their clothes from getting dirty at work. Manual workers always wash or shower after work, going to and from work in civilian clothes, carrying their snack and lunchpack with them in a brief-case. They are fastidious compared to English-speaking workers.

Clean outside too

If an Englishman's home is his castle, as used to be stated in every textbook, a German's castle is his garden. Like everything the sometimes pocket-handkerchief-sized gardens are tended with meticulous care. They look immaculate, like the insides of the houses themselves.

As a significant part of the south is mountainous, many of the tiny gardens are made delightful with Alpine plants.

Business Relationships

An early start

In Germany everything begins very early in the morning and finishes fairly early in the afternoon. It may take you some time to get used to German work routine. There is no tea break, and the lunchbreak is often only 30 minutes long. The degree of dedication to work depends upon the type of work and, of course, on the individual concerned, as everywhere.

9
Closer Relationships

Introduction: being a foreigner
'When in Rome, do as the Romans do', is particularly apposite when living in Germany. It is not that Germans expect you, as a foreigner, to conform slavishly to local customs. Provided you don't disturb people (see *Noise abatement*, p59 and the *Hausordnung*), no-one cares what you do within the four walls of your own home. However English-speaking people, especially British and American, often find it hard to accept that they, and not the local inhabitants, are the foreigners. This may sound absurd, but the message behind it is relevant. Some people forget that they are visitors to a foreign country and as such are foreigners themselves. Germans (and, one wants to say, despite the war) are not patriotic or even particularly nationalistic any more but they *are* sufficiently attached to it to resent a blatant disregard or lack of respect for their own way of life. Examples that spring to mind include a group of British students who celebrated Guy Fawkes' Night with a bonfire, noise and carousing without alerting the neighbours beforehand as to what was about to happen; and American students celebrating the 4th of July in front of their German student hostel without asking permission to do so.

Of course, awareness of foreign status goes deeper than that, but it need not be exaggerated by going to the opposite extreme and trying to become more German than the Germans or Bavarian than the Bavarians. It is a question of finding a happy medium.

Understanding Germany
Many aspects of the German way of life can be explained explicitly but can only be understood implicitly from the history and culture of the country. Otherwise you risk rejecting different customs without understanding why they are different.

Germany has *never* really been one country — its history has

Closer Relationships

been marked by different struggles to obtain unity, for religious and ethnic reasons. Bismarck achieved Prussian hegemony in 1871 but even under Hitler, who ruled the country with an iron fist, provincial loyalties remained very strong — as they are to this day. Today, of course, Germany is divided between West and East. Religion is still a political force to be reckoned with, mainly in the Catholic south in Bavaria but also (though less) in the Protestant north. Above all, the industrial revolution occurred much later in Germany, which until 1918 was essentially an agricultural — one could say partly feudal — society, with many petty princes ruling semi-independent states. Democracy came later with the Weimar Republic and was destroyed by Hitler. The last war brought ruin. The Federal Republic is the most recent and, it would seem, successful attempt to guarantee the rights of citizens *vis-à-vis* the State.

Germans have always had someone holding them down. Put more euphemistically, they are accustomed to being 'controlled' (*kontrolliert*). Until recently they didn't know what freedom meant. And it is this being controlled, being ordered about and being answerable to some local ruler or authority with the power of life and death that has left its imprint on the orderly disciplined always-by-the-book way that things are done.

People had their rights taken away legally under Hitler. Now rights are enshrined in the law, be it in the Bill of Rights (*Grundgesetz*) or other laws. They have democratic laws, but lack the tradition which goes with them. Consequently, to a very great extent, they live by-the-book and it may take some time for a long stayer to understand and accept this attitude.

German humour
Some people claim that it does not exist or that if it does, it is very strange. This is nonsense. Germans do have a sense of humour, but it is possibly more cerebral and expressed differently to that of the Anglo-Saxons. An English sense of humour is appreciated by Germans as being particularly dry (*trocken*), but their own brand of humour tends to be less dry and subtle and more direct, even physical. Humour is taken seriously in Germany — there are scholarly volumes on the subject — but things that English-speaking people would not find at all funny, such as when someone falls over, drops something, or something

goes wrong, Germans would laugh at. Furthermore there is the so-called *Schwarzer Humor* ('black humour') a mixture of the tragic and the comic.

However, laughing at the same things, sharing the same jokes, helps a lot, especially in a foreign country. Germans do not always understand British or American brands of humour; they don't understand horseplay or smutty jokes. There is no equivalent of 'rugger' songs. The social background is different; the associations are missing. Get to know someone first before trying out the full range of your humour, otherwise a friendship could easily be spoilt. What you find funny a German may not — indeed quite the reverse because he or she could take what you said as a joke seriously. Never, for example, ask someone who is fidgeting (and Germans tend to fidget a lot, or all talk at once, or talk to each other when someone else is speaking) whether they have ants in their pants. They will be most insulted! The British habit of winking to express a shared joke or understanding, is not understood as such and may well be misunderstood, especially by women. In any case Germans seem to find it very difficult to wink!

The saving grace in most situations is that Germans, when they realise you are British and are trying to crack a joke, will make an exception and laugh, even if the joke is not seen. This can misfire if your listeners laugh when you haven't tried to be funny.

One can only repeat; be careful! A misunderstood joke can spoil an evening or indeed a whole relationship. Know your German friend before trying to be funny. However, you must be prepared for people laughing in situations where you wouldn't. It is a question of different ranges of sensitivity.

Sadly, Germany is not a country where you can smile at people in the street whom you do not know and expect them to smile back. Life is too serious for that; people are not used to being smiled at by strangers; some other motive is assumed.

The importance of the written word
It may be difficult for an English-speaking person to appreciate in Germany the importance of the written word. There is a different attitude to paper. People are loath to commit themselves

on paper or once they do, in official quarrels, one can sense them putting on their armour.

Local attitude to foreigners

Cultural shocks can work both ways; what the foreigner thinks of living in another country and what the local inhabitants think of the foreigner. English-speaking long stayers are on the whole welcome, although it would be misleading to claim the American troops always are. Germans are not overtly racist and officially go to great lengths to avoid any suspicion of colour prejudice. However, in small town night clubs American GIs are not welcome, blacks in particular. In more sophisticated circles, for example at university, no such distinctions are made and on the whole most Germans distinguish between GIs and their officers. However, there is still much work to be done, in addition to what has already been achieved, to improve relations between American troops and the German populace. One gets the general impression that the Tommy is welcome although this depends upon how he behaves. Germans, in general, have a soft spot for the British, especially for Scots — particularly in the south for historical reasons — and they rarely distinguish between British, New Zealanders and Australians, though they do have some difficulty in understanding Antipodean speech.

Society

As in most developed industrial nations, the West German working class has shrunk in proportion to society as a whole. In the mid-1970s the lower middle class constituted 40.3 per cent of the population. Of increasing importance as a social-ethnic group are the so-called *Aussiedler* and *Heimkehrer*, that is, Germans living outside Germany, usually in communist-bloc countries, sometimes in territory eg parts of present-day Poland that once belonged to Germany. These people return to the Federal Republic, sometimes with a poor knowledge of German and little or no money and, tragically on occasion, with little prospect of gainful employment without considerable retraining. Added to this are politically persecuted refugees called *Verfolgte*, and the *Wirtschaftsflüchtlinge* — those seeking to escape poverty at home, usually Third World Countries.

In order to obtain refugee status the latter claim that they

Closer Relationships

are persecuted; sometimes they are successful, sometimes not. A *Wirtschaftsflüchtling* with determination and a means of support can remain up to two years in the Federal Republic before exhausting the entire legal appeals procedure. Many Germans, and especially the new right-wing Republican and the old NDP parties, feel that this is too long and that such bogus refugees should be got rid of sooner.

There are very mixed feelings among the public about accepting so many virtual foreigners (*Aussiedler* and *Heimkehrer*) or refugees (*Wirtschaftsflüchtling*) back into a country that already has pressure on housing and accommodation, and an uncomfortably high rate of unemployment.

This problem is particularly acute with the approximate 4.5 million immigrant workers (*Gastarbeiter*) who, in the large cities sometimes exceed 20 per cent of the local population and who frequently refuse to integrate into local society and thus form ghettos. This is especially so of the Turks who are often poorly educated and thus find it difficult to relinquish their Moslem culture in favour of the German way of life. This applies particularly in matters of education and the status of women who are barely emancipated in Turkey and not much more so in Germany. None of this need concern the English-speaking visitor, however.

Getting to know Germany is getting to know Germans and this means peeling away layers, mainly the 'Sie' down to the 'Du' layer. You can work in a German organisation (company or university) without really establishing contact with a colleague and then suddenly, perhaps in a chance meeting, it comes after fifteen years!

Though Germany may be a country of extremes and Germans have a penchant for the extreme, human relationships can take an unconscionable time to establish. You must be very patient. It is easy to give up in disappointment or frustration, return home in a huff and say that there are unbridgeable gaps between the two attitudes to life. And then comes the moment of understanding and acceptance.

Conversely Germans who live in England also experience the sudden flash of understanding and acceptance. I could give examples that would make this clear but because they would be very personal and betray confidences, I can only say that I have experienced acceptance. Yet I know several fellow countrymen who never will reach this stage however long they live in Germany; they are really in exile. Insight and patience, together with a knowledge of the language, are what makes for success in a long stay in Germany.

German manners

When I first came to Germany I found it difficult to adjust; people banged into me by mistake and did not automatically apologise; they didn't ask me to do something, they told me to do it, and they didn't always say 'thank you' afterwards. For example, don't expect to receive a gesture of 'thanks' when you give way to someone in traffic or on a country road. In banks, shops, or elsewhere you will be interrupted with a brief 'excuse me' and the person dealing with you will be called away.

People who telephone you never bother to announce themselves or apologise for disturbing you day or night. There are countless examples. The first thing to realise is that German manners are different. They are either formal and elaborate, such as giving someone precedence upon entering a room in an office — the decision as to who goes first can cause several seconds' dithering — or they are informal and, one feels in the English-speaking sense, non-existent. The latter is expressed in the language.

The 'polite' English 'Would you mind signing this?' 'Would you please sign this?' to get someone to sign a piece of paper is missing. You say 'Unterschreiben Sie bitte' ('Sign please') or 'Sie müssen hier unterschreiben' ('You must sign here'). Do *not* be offended, as some English people sometimes are; it is not meant discourteously. You just use the language in a different way. People aren't asked to do something as a favour when they must do it anyway — sign a document or carry out some duty or order. It is significant that in German those who want someone else (a colleague) to do something will say: 'Ich habe eine Attacke auf Sie vor' ('I've something planned against you'). It's a humorous way of explaining that you want someone to do something.

The corollary is that people, especially junior people, professor's assistants, are rarely thanked for having done something. It isn't considered necessary. The wretched person has merely

Closer Relationships

done the job he or she was paid to do. Again no discourtesy is intended.

Britishers may find such manners strange but there are situations where Germans are far more courteous than English-speaking people.

First of all on the telephone in business; usually you don't call someone and then start discussing the matter in hand, but begin by asking after the other person's health and *then* get down to business. You always say 'Don't mention it' (*'Bitte sehr'* or *'Bitte schön'*) when thanked for doing something. Women will often get up from their desks or chairs whilst in England they remain seated. German women are more emancipated in this respect. As to be explained in Chapter 17, a gentleman always enters a restaurant before the lady. When visiting someone's home, the host or hostess invites the guest to enter a room first. So far as I can gather through many years of observation the German male rarely accords a woman the same degree of outward respect as in English-speaking countries, but perhaps they treat them more as equals. Courtesy (*Höflichkeit*), as such, is regarded as a formality and less as an aspect of kindness. (The word *Hof* means 'court' and *Höflichkeit* derives from behaviour at court.) Kindness (*Freundlichkeit*) is more personal, between people you know well, and here kindness and courtesy merge. You'll find this quality occurs more frequently at the official level in English-speaking countries.

Life in Germany can be personal or impersonal depending upon age, occupation and predilection. As a foreigner you will necessarily become more occupied with the official bureaucratic *Sie* side of things which, if not properly organised, can waste an incredible amount of time, and less with the *Du*, more personal, friendly side. Therefore it pays to think things out well in advance. Take nothing for granted; it doesn't mean that Germans are unfriendly at the *Sie*-level, they just tend to be more impersonal.

Patience is an essential quality, to make a go of it in Germany; patience with ways of doing things you do not understand (tolerance is the better word, but sounds arrogant because *you* are the visitor), and patience to hold on in situations where mutual understanding in relations with a German takes considerably longer to develop than it would back home.

A friend of mine told me when he first came to Germany that he was frightened. It could have been a hangover from the war. Germans are so busy that they seem to have no time to relax nor even to pass the time of day. My experience is that they *are* kind and helpful once they realise that you are a foreigner.

Because of past history, wars, Third Reich, currency reforms, etc (mentioned above), and the older generation losing all its money twice, Germans are cautious even now to the verge of mistrusting each other. There is not the same degree of immediate trust based, for example, as in England, upon belonging to the same social group. In any case as a foreigner you are unlikely (at least to begin with) to belong to a sports club or social club (*Verein*) that will give entrée to local society.

Germans usually make an exception when dealing with foreigners, especially English-speaking ones. They spoil Britishers — at least that is my experience — less so Americans, with whom they have a different relationship. For Germans, Britishers are still polite and friendly, rather old-fashioned perhaps but generally to be trusted and respected. It is a shame to spoil this image however inaccurate. Soccer hooliganism has done untold harm in this respect but Germans believe that the phenomenon of hooliganism is very much determined by the hooligan's underprivileged social background — unemployment etc, conditions that mercifully do not pertain in their own country to the same extent.

Social attitudes

The ladder of social success is career and money orientated. Anyone can get to the top, but it tends to be via university, assuming the necessary ability. Education up to the highest level is free, that is State-aided. Social hierarchies are structured within the different professions and in ascending order according to income. Genteel poverty does not exist. The term 'genteel' is impossible to translate into German and the term 'gentleman' very difficult. In fact one uses the English word. Essentially, Germany is a classless society.

Those who object to old-fashioned English social mores should find life in Germany very refreshing.

Class-indicators such as speech and dress hardly exist. Speech, that is accent, varies according to the region and has little or nothing to do with class. There is no equivalent to the old City bowler hat and whangee-handed umbrella, no gentlemen's clubs, old school ties and the rest. There is no Ascot, MCC, or Wimbledon. True, German equestrianism is presented as in England, but there are no hunts like the Quorn (fox hunting is forbidden). Two world wars and the abolition of the monarchy have levelled down social differences. There are no 'ruling classes' or Establishment in the British sense of those terms, however inaccurate they may be. It all reflects essentially a thrusting middle class society, believing in a straight, no-nonsense approach to life.

The people who have the 'say' (*das Sagen haben*) tend to be either very few and elevated or in general in the civil service. There is a large number of lawyers in the civil service. A high proportion of civil servants are members of the *Bundestag* (German lower house of Parliament).

Social life
The good thing about German social life is that you can therfore please yourself. You do not *have* to turn up to this or that occasion. You can opt out, especially if you are the wife of an official.

If you do decide to attend receptions, grand affairs at national or local level, then be prepared to listen to long speeches and be able to absorb boredom. Official events and publications are not designed to be necessarily interesting either to the participator or reader. They are supposed to be objective and serve a purpose of being so. An anniversary event, to celebrate say the founding of a university, will consist of an item of music, prize-giving and several speeches. It is an ordeal for those attending. A dissertation by a professor's assistant, upon which the author's future career depends, is serious and objective to a degree and usually, although it has to be published afterwards, will be read by no-one apart from a few specialists. People seem afraid to make interesting speeches or write exciting academic publications because then they would not be taken seriously and thus not serve their purpose. This results in considerable wasted effort on everybody's part.

No doubt it is wrong to generalise, but I find that Germans are so serious that they lack a light touch; humour is definitely not part of the deal. They seem to appreciate the ritual of long speeches, and are enthralled by the commonplace generalities that make up a speech. It is nothing for a university professor to give a 3-hour lecture with, of course, a break in the middle, but still 3 hours! The witty after-dinner speech is unknown in Germany.

One wonders how private parties can go on for hours longer than seems necessary, but then they wouldn't do so if people weren't enjoying themselves. Germans have, to say the least, great social stamina. They can sit for hours and talk (and, one feels, never say anything). It is as though they gain reassurance from each other's company.

The whole business of socialising differs from the British social scene. The sherry party, the small talk, the moving quickly from person to person, from group to group with a word here and a word there, does not exist because people usually sit down, and sitting down means staying put. You may well be wedged in between two country bumpkins with whom it is almost impossible to strike up a conversation, and the awful thing is you cannot escape.

I introduced the idea of a sherry party for my students; their professor asked me what a sherry party was, to give a lecture on the subject and then to open it! He couldn't understand when I explained the first essential was to relax. If you are invited to someone's home for drinks or a buffet, you may have to stand with everybody listening to a speech of welcome from the host. This explains why some British expatriates get very drunk very quickly at German parties — it's self-preservation!

There is no compulsion to go. If you enjoy it, fine; if you don't, you have only yourself to blame, which seems perfectly fair. Both the gregarious and the loner can please themselves.

Titles

Titles are important in German society and business circles, and one uses them more than in English-speaking countries. Aristocratic titles were abolished as social titles following the 1918 revolution, but were incorporated into the name. *Count* Tannenburg would be known as *Graf* Tannenburg. Academic titles are recognised as part of the name; (*Professor*) *Dr* Schmidt is known as *Dr* Schmidt. The *Graf* and the *Doktor* are legally part of the respective person's name. Both sign their names with their respective titles. Professor is not an academic title, but refers to an academic's position. Most professors have doctorates and it is this title alone that appears on the passport. Academic titles are supposed to be taken more seriously in the south than in the north, but it would appear they are accorded universal respect, certainly far more so than in English-speaking countries. At present official steps are being drawn up to distinguish between the different types of professor, that is the university professor (*Universitätsprofessor*) who is an official of the State, and professors of *Fachhochschulen* (technical colleges) and *Akademien* (academies) as well as in some schools.

The long stayer should take titles seriously for diplomatic reasons. Most title-holders appreciate one using them at least on being introduced. After getting to know you, he or she may well say 'Don't bother'. Members of the former aristocracy expect one to use their titles out of courtesy.

The role of women

The pictures of women, young and middle-aged, clearing away the rubble at the end of the war with literally their bare hands, are unforgettable; the so-called 'Trümmerfrauen', now in their seventies, who lost husbands and sons in the war, kept their bombed homes going and then at the end of the war buckled to and, scarves on their heads, cleared away what remained of the bombed buildings. The women bore the brunt of the bombing, their menfolk were at the front, prisoners of war or dead. Hitler's last soldiers — the so-called *Volksturmm* were children and old people.

It is interesting to see the transition over the years between those who helped lay the foundation for Ludwig Erhard's *Wirtschaftswunder* (economic miracle) and today's young, well-groomed businesswomen; then see old women in the countryside wearing peasant costume for shopping or working in the fields as their forbears did in the past. Of course, it was women who so ecstatically welcomed the Führer, but they certainly paid for it.

Women as a group have risen like a latter-day Phoenix from the ashes of male domination and prejudice; this is a phenomenon of recent years.

German men used not to help with dishwashing or with the

cooking, but they are learning to now. With the high rate of male unemployment, many women go out to work and the husband looks after the children. But this happens in other countries too. There are, however, certain jobs where women are not employed. The great problem for mothers at work is care of the children. Some people expect mothers to stay home and look after their children, others consider this unnecessary where the authorities (*Länder* or municipal government) provide nursery school facilities. Recently a female CDU Minister for Social Services, Professor Ursula Lehr, shocked many members of her own party by arguing that there should be more facilities to enable mothers of two-year-olds to work.

Women long stayers: the position of women in German society

Single women making a home in Germany will find a society that accepts the idea of feminine emancipation without putting it completely into practice. Women are not always allowed to assume positions of authority at work. It is misleading to generalise but it would appear that while society is prepared to benefit from women filling middle and low rank positions, it is not prepared to allow women to climb much higher.

There are few female federal ministers or judges, university professors or managing directors (only 3 per cent in top management). However, in the lower courts, at school, in the middle and lower ranks of the Civil Service, in commerce and industry women are found to be indispensable.

The main source of grievance is that women rarely receive the same pay as men for virtually the same work. Women do more than half of the work in Germany and yet are paid on average only two thirds of what men receive. The usual reasons given to justify this unfair state are: women get married, have babies and are thus not considered so reliable as men; women cannot do such hard work as men, require more help etc.

According to Article 3 of the Basic Law (*Grundgesetz*) women are equal, but in 1984 men were paid a gross hourly wage of DM 16,59 in 'private industry' and women DM 12,00. 'Even skilled women earned less than untrained men.' In the same year the average gross monthly salary for men in commerce and industry was DM 4,025 and DM 2,725 for women. In government, however, men and women have equal salaries and wages.

Whilst women performing the same work as men are entitled to equal pay, that typically done by women ('physically lighter' work) is paid less than men's work. Higher up the scale, the so-called vocational jobs, the plum positions seldom go to women. Forty per cent of students are female but only 20 per cent of doctoral theses are written by women.

The result of such wage discrimination is that women find it easy to get lower paid jobs, such as hairdressing, but harder to find better paid manual jobs of the kind usually done by men, eg motor mechanic or dental technician. According to a recent European Community study, this is not only because of different qualifications or hierarchical considerations but because of subjective and discriminatory ones. Moreover women are under-represented in the *Bundestag* in particular, and in politics in general.

There are no uniformed women police but, on the other hand, and which is very sad, there have been some women terrorists, such as Astrid Poll and Ulrike Meinhof. Women are particularly active in social work, a fact that is largely unrecorded. Female emancipation is more pronounced among the young, but even older women are becoming increasingly aware of their equal rights.

The position of the single woman in Germany varies little from that in most English-speaking countries. In Germany there are many one-parent families.

The single woman in Germany, be she unmarried or a divorcee, is accepted as such socially and at work without any sort of discrimination, assuming that she has sufficient education and qualifications to do a reasonably well-paid job. Where material difficulties arise is when single women (German and foreign) in particular married or unmarried mothers, are not qualified to do even secretarial work but must rely for their livelihood on waitressing, cleaning and the like. This can be fairly lucrative when you are young and even remain so as you get older (there is always a shortage of reliable staff), but eventually hard physical work begins to tell on the back and sheer physical exhaustion on the nerves too. It's not easy. You must have qualifications for a less physically demanding job, and if you do not have them, think ahead and obtain them while you are still young (see *Divorce*).

(*Above*) Hamburg: Little Alster and the Alster Arcade (*Tourismus-Zentrale Hamburg GmbH*). (*Below*) The Mosel (*German Tourist Office*)

Berlin: (*above*) The Breitscheidplatz. Beside the Europa Centre, built on the site of the famous Romanische Cafe and nicknamed 'Powder-box and Lipstick', are the remains of the old Kaiser-Wilhelm-Gedachtniskirche (*Berlin Tourist Office*). (*Left*) Bric á brac market in the Zille Yard (Fasanenstraße) (*Berlin Tourist Office*)

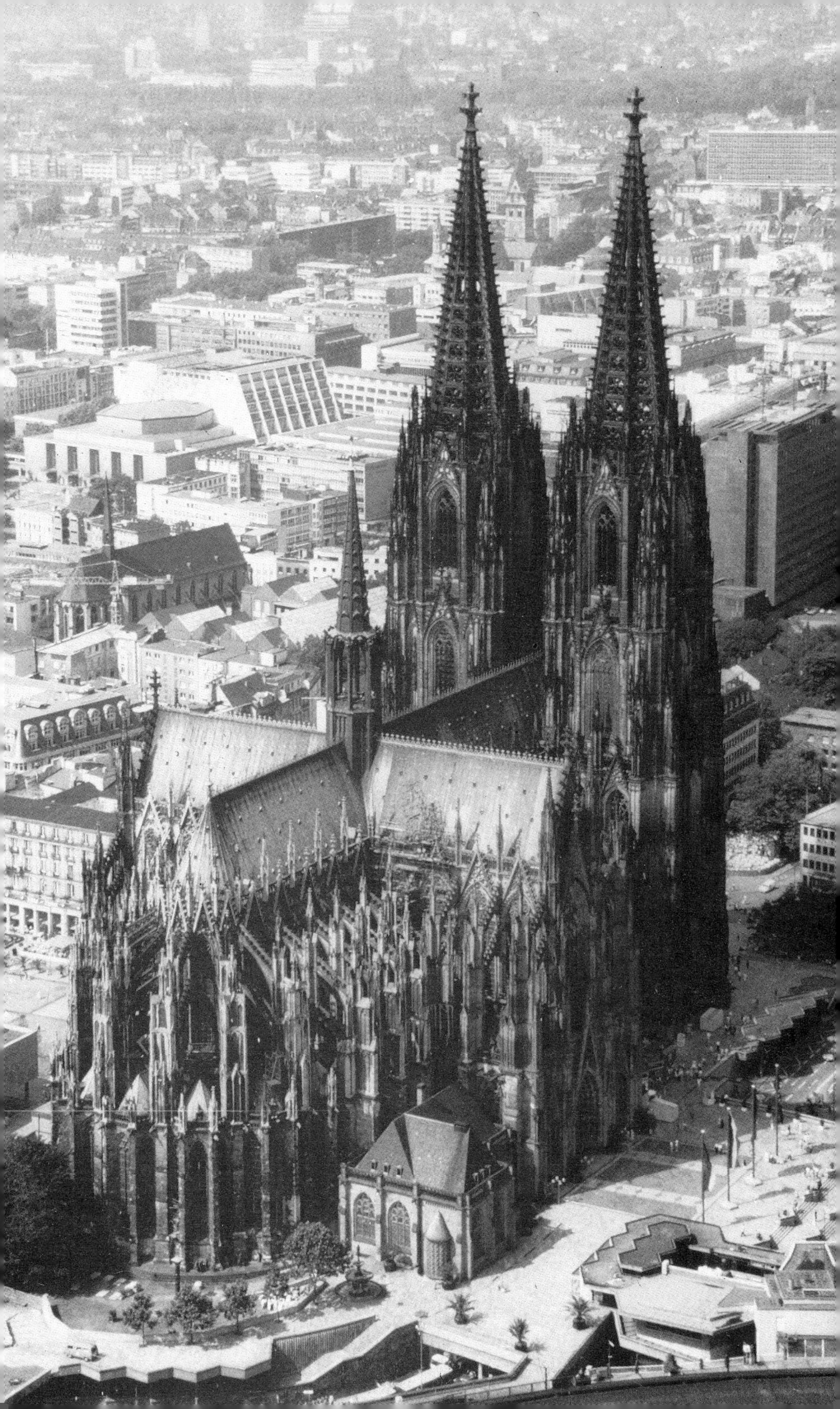

Bamberg: (*above*) The old Guildhall afloat in the middle of the river! In fact there are connecting bridges to both banks (*Bamberg Tourist Office*). (*Right*) The famous *Bamberger Ritter* (Bamberg Knight) in the Cathedral. Nobody knows whom he is supposed to represent (*Bamberg Tourist Office*)

Closer Relationships

If you cannot speak and write German your scope is necessarily limited unless you possess special skills such as teaching English, nursing etc, which are at a premium and do not require knowledge of the language. Local job centres (*Arbeitsämter*) will help, if they can, but citizens of non-Common Market countries should first enquire whether or not they are permitted to work more than a certain number of hours a week.

Marriage: marrying a local?

This book cannot deal with specific cases. Marriage is a personal matter between two people, but when different nationalities are involved certain practical questions arise. They relate to matters such as citizenship, taxes, pension and property rights. The couple may, of course, postpone the decision of whether or not to apply for German citizenship, or one party may already be a German citizen.

The marriage ceremony is conducted by a State official (*Standesbeamter*) at the Registry Office (*Standesamt*) and then afterwards, if desired, the marriage solemnised in church. Only the civil ceremony has any legal validity.

Marriage being an official State act at a registry office (*Standesamt*) and thus governed by a special law (*Ehegesetz*), some people draw up pre-marriage contracts so that the *Ehegesetz* does not apply to certain material and social aspects of their marriage (*Gütertrennung*). For example, the future husband might try to ensure through a private contract, that in the event of divorce while childless, he is not liable for alimony. However, the courts' acceptance of the validity of private pre-marriage contracts relating to alimony depends upon the particular situation pertaining after divorce. The future wife might insist upon the right to continue with her professional career even if she has children. Basically it is a question of getting things straight beforehand and reducing State interference.

According to the 1982 statistics, between 1 and 2.5 million people were living together without being married. So between 1972 and 1982 this group had increased by 27 per cent. According to a survey, 33 per cent of those undergoing a trial marriage intended to marry in the future; 38 per cent were still uncertain and 28 per cent did not intend to marry. Some

70 per cent of unmarried couples regarded the 'Zusammenleben ohne Trauschein' (living together without marriage licence) as a sort of engagement. Students did not want to lose their grants (*BAFöG*) which they would if they married. The group of older unmarried couples would lose certain pension rights if they married. The number of one-parent families has increased as elsewhere in the Western world.

Many couples live together unmarried, apparently over a third in the 18–35 age group, and this proportion seems to be increasing annually. 'Was habe ich von dem Trauschein?' ('What use is a marriage certificate?') young people ask, with a certain amount of justification when it comes to enjoying a relationship without the constraints of the whole gamut of legal liabilities and responsibilities which the institution of marriage involves.

Simply living together without being married obviously has its advantages but it also has disadvantages so far as enjoying various State benefits is concerned.

Taxes are levied individually — no advantages of dual husband and wife rates; gifts during both partners' lifetime or legacies after death from the deceased to the remaining partner enjoy less tax relief. The real complications arise for the couple when there is issue. The parents of an illegitimate child can marry and thus retrospectively legitimise their child's birth status. If they remain unmarried the child automatically becomes a ward of the Youth Department (*Jugendamt*) which acts as its guardian (*Vormund*). The *Jugendamt* is responsible for establishing the identity of the child's father and regulating the latter's financial duty to his child. The mother can apply to assume guardianship care (*Sorgerecht*) for the child and this will be granted by the *Vormundgericht* (Court of Guardians) if it is considered in the child's best interests. When the father acknowledges the child as his own he assumes financial responsibility for it and the child can inherit the same share of the father's estate as if it were legitimate, but only in terms of its share of the cash value of the estate and not a physical share of the same property. The *Sorgerecht* remains with the mother. She decides about schooling, choice of first names and religion for her child. The child may not use both his parents' names as a double surname (*Doppelname*) but only the mother's.

German names
Müller (in English, Miller) is the most common name in Germany (some 600,000), with slightly more than Schmidt (Schmidt, Schmitt, Schmid) and Meier (also spelt Mayer, Meier, Meyer). Whilst a married woman used to take her husband's name, a woman now often retains her maiden name or adds it to her husband's, thus a Fräulein Bauer marrying a Herr Schmidt may call herself Bauer-Schmidt.

Having a baby
Whilst the mother is fully involved in having a baby, the father may find the visiting hours, especially if he has a job, rather inflexible and the bureaucracy involved in registering the birth somewhat deflating. Obviously it depends on the hospital and on the registrar, but it is as well to be prepared for anything, or at least for something more complicated than would normally happen at home. Be especially careful that the registrar is familiar with the English spelling of the Christian names chosen, otherwise you may think your newborn child is called Elizabeth, and find Elisabeth on the birth certificate, or as a surname Philipps, instead of Phillips! You should also register the child's birth with the nearest home consulate to safeguard its nationality, whilst also being eligible for German citizenship.

Divorce
The twofold aim of the new divorce law (1977) has been to ensure that the old criterion of one party assuming responsibility for failure of the marriage and thus, as the guilty party, having to pay alimony has been changed to make the amount of alimony payable dependent upon the need of the other partner. If the divorced wife can work, and it is not unreasonable to expect her to do so, the amount of alimony paid by the husband is correspondingly less or not paid at all. Of course the cost of the upkeep and education of any children of the marriage is taken into consideration, but even with children, it can be expected sometimes that the wife should work half-time. The whole idea is to achieve more equality for the man *vis-à-vis* the woman when it comes to alimony and, at the same time, underlines the new rights of the woman to stand on her own feet. It is no longer a question of making the wicked ex-husband expiate his guilt by

paying so much alimony that his freedom to marry again and raise another family is strictly curtailed.

However, if the mother cannot support the children, the father is expected to pay towards their upkeep. The rights of the children are as follows: children have a statutory right to be supported by their parents. If a father refuses to help with financing his child's education, the latter can take the former to court. An example might be a father whose income is such as to make the child ineligible for a university grant who refuses to support his child at university. Recent legislation has been enacted to provide greater freedom for children from parental control whilst emphasising parental duty to care for offspring.

Children's world
Hitherto I have always regarded Germany as an eldorado for children and pets, but a colleague of mine feels that pets have a better deal than children. She pointed out that children always seem to be sitting meekly in restaurants and pubs rather than rushing around tearing the place down. My experience is quite different. Some thirty years ago, particularly in the north, children were exceedingly well behaved and gave the impression of being trained animals with their neat bows (the girls curtseyed to grown ups), but those days are past. Children leave the table when they will without asking permission and career around it. They seem to be as well- or ill-behaved as other children. The stress comes later when they go to school and they are urged by ambitious parents to get good marks. In their younger years they seem perfectly free, perhaps too much so.

10
The Language

Whilst German may seem a very difficult language to learn at first, you are certainly not confined to silence until you have learnt it. Most Germans know some English and are uninhibited about trying it out. Indeed, sometimes it is an advantage not to speak the language because Germans tend to accompany rudimentary English with a compensatory act of extraordinary kindness not accorded a fellow countryman. A German customs officer once opened the frontier post early in the morning for me before the official time.

You may find that the linguistic skills of most Germans in speaking English are a serious impediment to learning German. It becomes so easy to converse in your own language that learning another one seems superfluous! You must make up your mind to learn German. Don't attempt too much at once but try and master a little every day. In that way it becomes manageable.

Here are a few useful phrases; I have distinguished between German as spoken in the north and in the south:

	In the north		*In the south*
all day	Guten Tag!	*formal*	Grüß Gott!
am	Hallo!	*informal*	Grüß Sie Gott!
			Servus!
pm	Guten Tag!		Grüß Gott
	——— no equivalent of 'good afternoon' ———
evenings	——— Guten Abend (good evening) ———
	——— Gute Nacht (good night) ———
	Auf Wiedersehen (goodbye)	*formal*	Auf Wiedersehen
	Tschüs (cheerio)	*informal*	Behüt' Dich Gott
	Dankeschön (thank you)	*formal*	Dankeschön
	Danke (thanks)	*informal*	Danke

The Language

When calling to someone you don't know or when wanting attention, whereas in English one says 'Excuse me, please', in German you simply say 'Hallo!'; it is not considered impolite.

German and English were originally the same language and the great difference is that German is inflected (the endings change with nouns and adjectives) and English is not. We no longer say 'ye olde shoppe'. Our nouns do not have different genders as in Latin or modern Roman languages. Finally, there is no distinction between 'you' (*sie*) and 'thou' (*du*). Consequently English is, apart from the idioms, much less complicated than German. In general, and up to a moderate level of competence, Germans find it much easier to learn our language than English-speakers do theirs.

This should not put you off going to Germany but language should be taken into consideration if you are to get the most out of the experience. Many poorly educated Turks and Italians live in linguistic ghettos because they do not bother to learn the language, as do some English and American people. If you can achieve a moderate competence in the language, the rewards of trouble-free communication are worth the effort. One of them is undoubtedly that the fact of being a foreigner (see p84) assumes less importance.

Official language

The style of spoken language is reflected in the written language. Commercial English tends to be wooden, but German business language, even when dealing with non-technical matters has no aspiration to literary merit. No German businessman tries to get his personality across when he writes officially; he is merely writing on behalf of his employer. He could be a robot, submerging his personality on purpose. British people, in particular, find this difficult to understand, especially in submitting applications to government departments. Always ask a German to help you fill in such applications to ensure you keep to a correct, impersonal form of language. Never, ever, crack a joke in a letter of application. It will not be appreciated and might even be seen as an ill-advised attempt to be facetious. There is no German equivalent of Sir Ernest Gowers' *Plain English*.

The Language

Learning the language to take part in local cultural activities

Whilst local English-speaking drama companies perform some English plays, most theatre is in German, which often consists of translations from English. Local theatre and opera is also mainly in German but don't allow yourself to be put off going because of the language. Otherwise you will lose out on a whole range of theatre and be reduced to relying on musicals or concerts.

The cinema and TV are a means of improving one's German. Some English films are shown in the original but usually they are dubbed. Film clubs, though, show original films.

Not only the verbal but also the written word is culturally important. You need to be able to read not only the German newspapers and magazines but also the literature.

A lot depends on how much *you* depend upon literature for spiritual sustenance. It is surprising how many English-speaking people (and highly intelligent ones at that) miss so much because they can't be bothered to learn the language. I know a Cambridge graduate, a writer and gourmet, who went into the catering business locally and denied himself the chance to rise to the top because he never learnt to write German fluently. He felt unsure of his written language and so never took the *Meisterprüfung* (cookery diploma) that would entitle him to train others. German is a difficult language, but to some degree it can be mastered.

There is no shortage of aids to learning the language; books, cassettes, video packs and so on, but best of all remains actually talking to Germans and using the language as well as learning it — see reading list at the end of the book.

Be careful when armed with a smattering of the language and the necessary confidence to use it; confusion can arise. For example, 'halb-sechs (Uhr)' means half-past five and not half-past six ie 5.30 and not 6.30; 'viertel-sechs' means 5.45 and not 6.15 which would be 'viertel nach sechs'. The best way is to always ask a German to confirm the time using the 24-hour clock so that there is no misunderstanding. In any case the 24-hour clock is often used. If you are told 'viertel-sechs', then make sure that 'viertel *vor* (before) sechs' is meant.

Another source of confusion lies in dates. An invitation

111

The Language

issued on Tuesday for 'nächsten Donnerstag' (next Thursday) does not mean in two days' time (that would be 'am kommenden Donnerstag'), but 'Thursday of next week'. The best thing is to check the actual date.

Beware too that Germans, even with a fair working knowledge of English, will often answer a question to which you expect the answer 'No' with 'Yes' when they mean 'No':

'So you won't come to supper on Thursday?'

'Yes' – which means 'No', ie he or she will not come.

Where bad language is concerned, Germans use anal as opposed to sexual expressions more than English-speaking people do and you get used to hearing it. I remember more than twenty years ago a friend had an English car. The local garage referred to the vehicle as 'a shit box' (*eine Scheißkiste*) which, when reported back to the British manufacturer, caused more consternation than was necessary. The expression in German is less provocative than in English when translated literally.

English-speaking people who translate German literally have the impression that Germans always order one another about when they say 'müssen' (must); for example, 'you must sign here'; this is not meant as an order at all. The point is grammatical; 'mussen' in German is used as a modal verb, like *can* in English. It may be used to express that something has to be done, but is also used where in English you might say: 'Would you mind doing something, please' – it is not meant imperatively at all. Some people would disagree with this interpretation and assert that when Germans say 'müssen' they mean 'must', and to some extent this is true because of the German attitude to authority. There is no need to exaggerate. 'Müssen' generally means that that is the way to do something and there is really no other way of doing it. The word is possibly just a more direct way to express oneself.

When having a disagreement with a German you may hear, 'Nein, das is falsch' ('No, that is wrong') whereas in English you might say: 'Well, you've certainly got a point, but I don't think it's quite like that.' I don't want to generalise, but Germans do tend to be more direct and when they are, it is *not* meant discourteously.

The Language

Conversely, when Germans say 'No' to a request, they often put it indirectly, like 'Das geht schlecht' ('That won't be easy') which means 'No'. Or they will say 'No' by not answering a letter or by postponing a decision. They can be masters of diplomacy in this way when dealing with fellow Germans, but they sometimes achieve the opposite of what is intended with English-speaking people and in trying to avoid giving offence, they appear not to care (see *Morals* p78).

11
Communication with Home: The Postal System

While most firms now have fax and other means of communication, the average long stayer, certainly in his home, will have to rely on the Federal Post Office (*Bundespost*) for overseas mail.

The Post Office is a microcosm of how German officialdom works and how complicated basically simple operations can be made. You can also spend considerable time at a post office waiting at one counter, then being sent to join a queue for another just to buy a few postage stamps to send letters home. Most moderately sized towns and cities have one late-night (*Spätschalter*) a week during which the post office is open for business but a late fee is levied on registered letters.

Considerable time can be saved by observing a few rules:

1. Look in the telephone book or get hold of a leaflet or booklet (*Postgebührenheft*) giving the various postal charges.
   Get someone to translate the main terms:
   Brief: letter
   Postkarte: postcard
   Briefmarke: stamp
   Gebühr: fee
   Eilboten: express
   Einschreiben: registered post
   Luftpost: air mail
2. Buy a pair of letter scales. There is a small one on the market which will weigh post up to 1kg.
3. Buy postage stamps in bulk from the post office in one fell swoop in the denominations customarily used and have your own little post office. It's worth becoming a postal expert.

Communication with Home

You will literally save yourself hours and no little frustration by posting your mail and avoiding countless visits to the post office.

The envelope is addressed as shown. The *Postleitzahl* (zip code) precedes the towns and should always be used. A list of zip codes can be obtained at the post office.

Herrn
Thomas Schmidt
Königsstraße 10

1000 Berlin 2

These examples show how involved German Post Office procedure can be:

Post Office Regulations: Sending Books

Although there is a special inland 'book rate', there is no official overseas 'book rate'. However, there is a special 'printed matter at reduced rate' (*Drucksache zu ermäßigter Gebühr*), which amounts to the same thing, but has also to be written in French on the parcel: *Imprimé à taxe réduite*, as well as German. No letter may be included, but if the book is a gift, you may indicate donor and recipient. Moreover, you are not allowed to secure the parcel with an ordinary knot. It pays to use special *Jiffy* bags. Books can be sent in a larger parcel up to 5kg at parcel rate and you can knot that parcel as usual, but parcel rate is extremely expensive, though you can reduce the cost slightly by sending it to UK via Hamburg as opposed to Cologne.

Sending valuables

In the unlikely event of having to send an insured parcel (*Wertpaket*), you are in for a major operation unless the following requirements are adhered to:
1. Do not use an adhesive label for the address, but write it on the wrapping paper.
2. If the contents involve customs inspection you will need to complete special forms and the contents must be shown to local customs before taking the parcel to the post office. The customs will examine the contents, seal the parcel with wire

Communication with Home

and you will then take the parcel to the post office where the wire is removed before despatch.
3. The parcel is then secured with one single piece of string and all knots etc, must be sealed with sealing wax and impressed with a signet ring. You can buy a sealing wax set, complete with signet ring, at any stationer's (*Schreibwarengeschäft*).
4. You then pay a small fortune to the post office! Advice: If you value your time more than the contents of the parcel, never send a *Wertpaket*! If you ever have to, and you read this book and taken the advice therein, you'll bless me. However if you are happy with insurance up to DM·490, you can send the *Wertpaket* unsealed.

Incidentally, Germans to do not lick postage stamps when sticking them to letters nor do they lick envelopes when sealing them. Post offices provide moistening pads at every counter.

Unlike the UK, post moves over the weekend. In many cities and some middle-size, even small towns, the main post office is open for a few hours on Sundays. Postboxes marked with a red circle have more frequent collections than the rest. Mail can be speeded up by using the red circled boxes or taking it to the main post office. Delivery within the Federal Republic is efficient. Usually you can post a letter in the evening in Nuremberg and it will be delivered the next day in Hamburg. Inland mail is carried by air overnight between the large cities. Inland mail is more expensive than in UK but because of the Common Market, it costs no more to send a letter first class from Munich to London than to Hamburg.

Dealing with the Post Office and the Customs

Dealing with Customs (*Zollamt*) demands patience. Try and avoid this 'Amt' as much as possible. The procedure for dealing with a parcel that has been through Customs is both costly and complicated. You'll curse the day Auntie Flo ever promised to send you a cake or, worse still, dutiable items like tea over 100g and coffee over 500g. Very briefly (though it will take far longer to complete the procedure) what happens is this: if there is no-one at home you receive an invitation on a brick red card to collect the parcel from the post office. If the bill is not inside (obviously not, in Auntie Flo's case) but the contents are dutiable, the post office will ask you to send in the bill. The Customs official will

Communication with Home

then refer to a list and bill you and you then pay the postman. If you go in person, you pay at Customs. It will be explained to you that what you are required to pay, should it emanate from a country within the Common Market, is not duty or customs at all but Value Added Tax (*Mehrwertsteuer*) which the sender should have been able to reclaim from his or her own government before despatch.

A parcel from America, Australia, Canada or Japan is also liable for import duty. Mercifully, books, up to a certain combined weight, are excluded. The same should be so, though in my experience not all customs officials know this, for research material, ie, Xeroxed copies or archival material. Again, dealing with Customs is an art and depends upon the local office. If it is plain sailing, the VAT will be levied by the postman who delivers the parcel, which will have been opened by the post office and examined by Customs. The VAT bill includes a postal charge of DM 2.50 for delivering the parcel. One legitimate way of avoiding all this is to send the contents, assuming the size allows, by letter post with a green customs label stuck on the envelope. The post office is then allowed to deal with the matter without reference to Customs. It's obviously difficult with Auntie Flo's cake, but she could just send flapjacks!

If you want a letter or parcel to arrive quickly from UK, have it sent 'Swiftair' to your private address during the week, but at the weekend or over a public holiday to the nearest airport customs marked 'to be called for' (*zur Abholung*). Then arrange with airport customs to collect it in person from them. Otherwise there will be a hold-up because your own customs office is closed and the packet cannot be released. 'Swiftair' letters do not usually go through Customs.

Telephoning
Telephoning in Germany is a skill well worth cultivating because, as explained, Germans take the written word very seriously. Over the 'phone you can achieve a great deal without putting pen to paper. Usually there are no witnesses. The other person is free to say what he or she wants. Many misunderstandings can be cleared up. At the same time personal and immediate confrontation does not take place. However, the call may serve as a useful introduction to a personal meeting.

Communication with Home

For most people it is easier to speak than to write in a foreign language. There is greater tolerance. The style of telephone conversation is in any case different. Usually you can work out over the phone how an application or particular letter should be worded.

Getting through to people in Germany is easier than in English-speaking countries because at work everyone — high and low — has a personal dial-through number so that it is rarely necessary to go through the exchange with all the waste of time and expense involved. You can establish whether or not someone is there simply by dialing the number. Of course, to talk to a senior executive you will go through the secretary, but this is faster than going through a central exchange.

You use the same vocabulary (see p109) on the phone as elsewhere, with one exception — when ending the conversation say 'Auf Wiederhören' (literally to the next 'hearing') instead of 'Auf Wiedersehen' (to the next seeing, ie meeting).

When making a social, or for that matter a business, call it is courteous to apologise for disturbing the person you are calling. In business your call often is a disturbance because German businessmen and officials, if they don't have a secretary or the secretary is away from her desk, cannot cut themselves off from the phone. It rings and they answer it — regardless of what is on hand.

Calling people at home can also cause inconvenience. Therefore the preliminary questions: 'Am I disturbing you?' ('Störe ich?') will be appreciated and be answered on occasion by a white lie: 'No of course not'. Germans are usually very understanding in this respect and show infinite patience. Many times I have called a German friend or colleague in desperation and have been reassured and helped. God bless the telephone! But don't abuse it. Calling people at home is an invasion of their privacy (see *Sie* and *Du*).

Keep your telephone number to yourself if possible. Telephone manners are not always what they might be. Make sure the number you are taking over was not formerly that of a business. A colleague of mine took over the number of the service department of a large mail order house and he was forever being rung up by anxious housewives wanting their washing machines and the like repaired. He complained to the manager

Communication with Home

of the mail order firm who said he wanted to use up the 5,000 notices with the old telephone number on them before having the next batch printed! Only when my colleague threatened to go to law did the manager see reason.

The telephone system, which has not been privatised, works well, but is more expensive than in the UK, though a cheaper tariff for phoning abroad within the Common Market has been introduced. A useful piece of advice is whenever you experience difficulty with Enquiries or/and with any telephone official, ask to speak to the supervisor (*Aufsicht*) and you will find that miracles will be achieved. The *Aufsicht* is usually most helpful.

12
Bureaucracy

Take bureaucracy seriously. The art of dealing with Germany is to master the small things of life, you ignore them at your peril! What seems so simple in English-speaking countries can become a major operation in Germany. What, in one's own country, is simple, such as receiving a registered letter or sending a parcel, can become fraught with loss of temper and time. Perhaps more than in any other Western country, in Germany it pays to know the regulations (*Vorschriften*): how to matriculate at a local university, deal with the post office, and so on. If you get things right, know which forms to fill in and what piece of paper or certificate to show when, then everything works like clockwork. Let one piece of paper be missing, then — and this is no exaggeration — it can be sheer unadulterated hell. I write from experience!

Der Beamter
At the heart of German bureaucracy is the *Beamter* (the official). Germans often admit that 'Germany is a country of officials' (*Beamtenstaat*) and it is true. One characteristic of the German labour scene is the distinction —mentioned earlier — between *Beamter* (officials) and *Angestellter* (employees). Now for a greater detail — a *Beamter* is a civil servant who has certain privileges (free contributions to the state pension scheme) and obligations (*Beamter* are not allowed to go on strike). *Beamter* are employed in government or municipal departments and nationalised industries as well as in the police and armed forces. There is a special procedure for becoming a *Beamter* which involves a probationary period before being *verbeamtet* (appointed). Only German citizens may become *Beamter*, though exceptions are made for certain senior professional people eg, foreign professors working at local universities.

Now for a few principles in dealing with bureaucracy!

Bureaucracy

First principle: you have to prove everything in writing
'Alles muß belegt werden' is a sentence you will often hear when dealing with officials. It is essential to realise that officially no-one is prepared to believe you unless you can prove in black and white what you say (see *Trust*). Hence the frequent necessity to show identity cards to prove your identity. Always be able to do this. The police are empowered to demand it. Always carry driving licence, insurance papers (the Green Card will do) and the *Kraftfahrzeugschein* (vehicle registration document) with you when driving, in case the police ask to see them. It could be very inconvenient if you don't have the papers with you. Also, take care to have the necessary certificates and stamped documents with you especially when applying for money, grants and the like. When filing a tax return it is doubly essential to be able to prove in black and white every single payment you have made, every expense you have had, in order to obtain tax rebates – see *Taxes*. It pays, in both money and time, always to be able to back up all verbal statements and every written claim. There is a premium on being efficient and punctilious. There is no 'Gentleman's-word-is-his-bond'-approach to life. If you protest, you will be told: 'Of course I believe you, but I am afraid I have to have the *Belege* (receipts) or have it in writing.' (Exceptions are made on occasion, but most unwillingly – and you cannot expect others to keep making exceptions, but must just get accustomed to a different approach to doing business.)

Second principle: 'I'm not responsible' –
'Ich bin nicht zuständig'
'Ich bin nicht zuständig' is a phrase you will often hear on first coming to Germany before you learn how to discover just who is responsible for what. Never assume that people are prepared to deal with anything that does not strictly concern them.
  This may seem at first rather wooden and unimaginative until you realise that the worst thing that anyone can do is poach someone else's work or responsibility. This system works so long as everybody is there. Usually there is a *Vertreter* (a deputy or representative) for absentees, but often the *Vertreter* will be unable or unwilling to take the decision in the absence of the person who is responsible. A particular matter I was involved with was held up for months because a secretary was ill.

Bureaucracy

I should add that the young lady was ultimately retired (or even sacked) but this provided no consolation. Her boss ultimately discovered that the relevant papers for which everyone was feverishly looking had been deposited in the wastepaper basket that happily had not been emptied for months! Always find out first who is responsible for a particular matter and then nail that person. Don't bother to explain the affair to a colleague. He or she may listen very carefully and courteously but then at the end will say: 'Terribly sorry, but it's not my business' — 'Ich bin nicht zuständig'. And you'll be obliged to repeat the whole story all over again to someone else. It could be, of course, that the business is so complicated that it is easy to work out who is responsible ('zuständig'). In this case it is worthwhile having a written summary available which, if it is not too confidential, you can show to different people who might then help you find the right person to deal with the matter.

Third principle: Find the right Beamter
You'll often see the wrong person first because the porter at the door or the receptionist will misunderstand you and suggest the wrong person. Work out your strategy before tackling a complicated matter with a government department. Telephone ahead to locate the right official and make an appointment with him or her for a specific time. The official will then have time to prepare for your visit.

Fourth principle: Master official etiquette!
Another vital word in official vocabulary is *Sprechstunde*, that is the consultation hour when every official is available for *Parteiverkehr*, when members of the public call on him to discuss business. The problem with the *Sprechstunde* is that one may wait a long time. Ask the official if it helps to come early or late, when the best time is likely to be. Sometimes the official may be gracious and suggest a *Sprechstunde* outside the normal hours.

You need to get used to the German system of having a *Besprechung*, an official talk, with someone. It is not just a conversation, but an interview that may well take place in a special room (*Besprechungszimmer*). You do not have an automatic right to speak to someone on business but are very much a petitioner; with luck you will find someone who will listen to your request (*Anliegen*) but it isn't always certain. People are busy. That is why it is better to ring up first and make an appointment.

Fifth principle: Don't underestimate the power of the administration

The importance of the administration (*Vertwaltung*) in any company or institution should not be underestimated. Everyone takes it seriously and indeed it has great power. English-speaking people are apt to come to Germany to take up a post, and make the mistake of ignoring administrative requirements, and then they wonder why things go wrong, various monies are not received and facilities aren't granted. The golden rule is: keep, read and file everything and if you don't understand something, ask and be sure to take whatever action is required. Having to undo what has gone wrong or been forgotten takes up an exorbitant amount of time that you can invest far more usefully elsewhere.

Moreover, by reading notice boards not only will you avoid missing things but you may also discover new ways to improve your position. Beware though; some activities, supported by the administration, are virtually a waste of time should you become too involved.

An example concerns becoming a *Vertrauensmann* (a counsellor) for foreign employees. There is one or more in each company or institution. The *Vertrauensmann* (it can also be a woman) attends meetings of the *Betriebsrat* (works council) without being officially a member. Although it is an honour to be appointed, this activity can take up much time in committee dealing with matters in detail and thus preventing you from getting on with your own work. Keep informed, but don't be drawn in too much.

Sixth principle: Beware the Verwaltungsakt

In government or municipal departments an official exercises great power when he effects a *Verwaltungsakt* (an official act) which is recorded in writing, duly signed and stamped. If done in your favour, all well and good, but if the opposite, you may need legal help to have it rescinded. You'll find examples when

Bureaucracy

applying for admission to university, for a grant, or much later for (German) citizenship. The main thing is to see that the *Verwaltungsakt* will be in your favour before the official makes his decision.

This is where personal diplomacy is important. Find out what the requirements are beforehand, but above all don't let anything come to a *Verwaltungsakt* until the ground has been prepared and the time is ripe.

Remember that administrative appeals on decisions cost money. A factory owner who applies for remission of a particular tax, makes due application and is informed that the official is likely to refuse, will withdraw the original application because a fee becomes payable if the appeal is presented and rejected. Withdraw the appeal and there is no fee, or be prepared to go to court. Unlike English-speaking nationals, Germans find no difficulty in making impersonal administrative decisions. What they frequently do find difficult is to relate such decisions to the people concerned. This has advantages and disadvantages. I was the subject of an administrative decision that affected me in a very personal way. The official who made the decision found this difficult to understand because, as he said, it was only a *Verwaltungsakt*. This had the disadvantage of making the official appear callous. However, by regarding the matter as being impersonally motivated, no-one loses face. This becomes a great advantage when the *Verwaltungsakt* is a decision in one's own, as opposed to the official's favour. Because it is a purely administrative decision, he need not take it personally. The aim is to make everything more objective or at least to appear so.

Eventually one sees administrative decisions as a game played out with each side appealing to rules and regulations, and you realise that the only way to win is to play the game according to the rules. Never appeal to an official's better nature or to a strictly moral approach, but always to the regulations (*Vorschriften*). This doesn't mean to say officials have no heart – they have; but to show their good intention there must be a *Vorschrift* which is applicable. Assuming you have kept your temper and have been diplomatic, officials will usually try to find a way to help, but bluster and you will be lost.

I have found it best always to take advice before letting it come to the *Verwaltungsakt*. Ask the official concerned first,

Bureaucracy

hypothetically, how it is likely to work out *before* making an application. Negotiate before anything is put down on paper. If you are unsure how things will go, don't ask for a decision, but seek the official's advice about the likely decision, were due application made. Generally the official will advise how best to approach the problem and it may be quite different from the way you had thought of going about it. Often, too, the official will explain how to write the letter of application, and suggest what might be better left out. I repeat: don't just charge in, never bluster nor make appeal to moral precepts, but remain cool and deliberate. If necessary read up the relevant *Vorschriften* in the library beforehand.

Stempel

Never forget the importance of the rubber stamp (the *Stempel*). Often a signature to a document is not enough, a *Stempel* is also necessary. Some business letters eg, from banks, are signed by two people. Some documents carry the signature of a senior person, the *Stempel* of his institution and a second signature certifying that the first signature is genuine. All this may appear strange to English-speaking people, but it is the established way of doing things.

It is difficult at first to accept that bureaucracy is taken so seriously, but it can be used to good account as the following story shows:

After giving lectures I arrived at the post office a few minutes before six, with ample time to go to the counter to send a letter by registered post. However, as luck would have it, there was snow on the ground and a motorist had difficulty in getting out of the parking space I wanted. I got out and helped the other motorist. He was grateful. It made me late at the post office and so the counter clerk demanded an extra fee. I dashed out, found the motorist I had helped and asked him for a chit explaining why I was late. Armed with this, I then returned to the post office and solemnly showed it to the post office official who smiled and excused me paying the fee on the registered letter at 6.02 pm. I have found that armed with the right piece of paper in Germany you can move mountains. Conversely without it the simplest things remain almost impossible. Take the example of trying to pick up a pile of second-hand toys for refugee children donated

125

Bureaucracy

by an English parish. The relevant customs official was at the dentist and couldn't complete the necessary release certificate. No-one in the whole customs department, including the official's supervisor, was able to do it. I had to wait for a long time. So get your paperwork perfectly prepared beforehand.

Bureaucracy in Germany is not just an institution but a state of mind that takes English-speaking long stayers quite a while to understand. Master it and forget it. Fail to master it and you are doomed to waste a lot of time in sheer unnecessary misery.

13
The Law: Under Constant Supervision

Even at the superficial and very visible level one is struck by the abundance of *Verboten* (it is forbidden) notices — indeed, how many things are forbidden, from walking on the grass (though admittedly this one is becoming less frequent) to smoking in a cinema.

Life is visibly far more strictly regulated (*kontrolliert*) than at home. There seems to be a law, regulation or paragraph to regulate every aspect of human activity. One professor told a colleague of mine that if you obeyed them all, you would go crackers! One third of the working population comprises officials, to see that these laws and regulations are observed — from the police to see that the average citizen keeps the peace, to the chimney sweep (*Kaminkehrer*) who sees that the chimney is unblocked or that the gas heater is working properly, to the *Feuerbeschauer* (fire officer) who checks that one does not have any inflammables in the cellar. All this, to some extent, is reassuring; for the newcomer on the other hand, it is unnerving, not to say a damn nuisance when at 6am there is a ring at the doorbell and the chimney sweep demands that you runs the hot water to see if the gas heater is working satisfactorily!

The police not only set speed traps but often check drivers' papers. As mentioned previously it is obligatory to have the driving licence in the car, ie on one's person. You must also carry your identity card (*Ausweis*). Foreigners should carry some form of identification. It's a nuisance to have to carry a passport but the police expect you to have it because of the *Aufenthaltserlaubnis* (temporary residence permit) stamped inside. After a time, British or European citizens may be issued with a European Community identity card (*EWG Ausweis*), which you should carry at all times.

All this is part of the German way of life, but you get used to it and after a while are glad that so many different people

The Law

take the trouble to ensure that everything is OK (*in Ordnung*). Everything must be *in Ordnung* otherwise people get confused. Everything must be done just right and this usually means in writing with signature and rubber stamp if it is to be official; if it is not official, it is worthless.

Daily life, therefore, becomes a game of observing (or getting round) the regulations or choosing the next best ones to observe, such as the example of a kindly post office clerk helping to find a cheaper way of sending bulky business papers to England.

Long stayers and the Law

You are unlikely to have active recourse to law assuming that you pay your bills promptly and live in peace with your neighbours and especially with your landlord, if you have one. However you may have recourse to law passively. A landlord or a tradesman sues for payment. It could well be that a mistake has been made. I was hounded to the point of almost being dunned for non-payment of a bill for services that were never rendered to me but to someone else! It can happen so easily in this day of computerised bill collecting. And it is very difficult to reason with a computer. Always keep receipts so that you can prove payment has been made for goods received and for services rendered. Otherwise you can find yourself manoeuvred into the ridiculous position of having to prove your innocence, ie, show that you didn't buy a book two years before, as happened to me once.

Going to law

Best avoid it. However, it is possible willy-nilly to be involved in a legal matter or even in a court case during a long stay in Germany, be it at work, buying a house, or possibly in appearing as a witness in court. These things happen. The law is very much part of many people's lives, much more so possibly than in English-speaking countries for the reasons given above. Whilst many Germans do not like going to court, an increasing number are going, if only because it is appreciably cheaper than in the UK or the USA. People can obtain legal cover from special insurance companies. For DM 200, I am covered for legal advice and representation in court for housing problems, labour matters,

The Law

income tax and so on. It has proved one of the best investments I ever made.

If you do have to consult a lawyer and use his services he may well charge up to DM 350 (£120) an hour! Others, depending upon the matter in hand, may charge appreciably less. Finding a good lawyer, like finding a good doctor, is in any country not always easy — personal recommendation is the best method — but once you have found one, hold onto him!

If you are in doubt, make enquiries first before choosing one. The nearest British Consulate usually has a list of local solicitors who have helped British citizens in the past. Some local solicitors specialise in working for English-speaking foreigners, but this isn't to say that they are the best lawyers. As in any country it is a matter of finding the lawyer most suited to the particular case.

The local court (*Amtsgericht*) also has a list of lawyers and a sympathetic court official may be able unofficially to suggest someone. I have found that some court officials are most sympathetic to foreigners. Not always, of course, but many like to practise their English and undoubtedly such enquiries make their otherwise routine job more interesting.

It is also advisable to have a car breakdown insurance arrangement with a German automobile association (*ADAC — Allgemeiner Deutscher Automobil-club*) or with a professional or trade union that provides such insurance facilities.

Trade Unions

I am conservative by nature and political persuasion yet would urge every long stayer to join at least one trade union. I am a member of three — as a teacher, an *Angestellter* and as a writer. The first one is rather left-wing but paid all my legal costs during a court case; the second one gave me advice and the third has given me accredited status as a journalist and will, I hope, protect my interests as a writer. I regard all three as an insurance policy. I have never yet had to man the barricades and recognise that unions are necessary institutions to protect the rights of the individual, not so much against the employer per se, but against the State. I leave it to you to decide whether or not to join one.

The Law

The nature of German Law

There is no equivalent to English Common Law and no distinction between Common and Equity Law ie, law that has developed as a result of precedents being corrected by appeals to the Crown. German law is contained in written laws essentially like English Statute Law, and contained in law books such as BGB (*Bürgerliches Gesetzbuch*). Cases are decided by reference to these laws, which sometimes offer difficulties in interpretation; then by precedent the decisions of higher courts govern the decisions of the lower ones.

The essential difference is that everything is written down. There is no oral tradition in court. There is no cross examination (*Kreuzverhör*), no distinction between barrister and solicitor, no Inns of Court, Bar, none of the ceremony and theatre that mark a trial at the Old Bailey. The prosecution in criminal cases is obliged to present both sides of the case, to consider an accused's possible innocence as well as probable guilt. The judge is not just a referee, as in England, but his own jury too, though in serious criminal cases he is assisted by two assessors (*Schöffen*), with whom he decides whether the accused is guilty or not. The judge represents the State. Although the judgement is handed down in the name of the people (*im Namen des Volkes*), in fact it is in the name of the State. Germans are very much governed by the State. They accord much more authority to it than would appear to be the case in the UK or the USA, although certain elements, criminal, terrorist and middle class Greens as well as other environmentalists do not hesitate to challenge the authority of the State.

14
Tips for Students

University matriculation
Those wishing to study at a West German university should make postal enquiry from home first to see which documents are required, because even if a place is available certain documents are required. This is assuming you have obtained the equivalent of *Abitur* ('A' levels or High School Diploma) which, in Germany, gives the holder a constitutional right to attend university, but not necessarily either the choice of subject or of university. In academic parlance, the *Abitur* is a *Reifezeugnis*, the required permit to attend university. The university administration will require the equivalent of this. Whereas Germans have to apply to the central admissions body in Darmstadt (*Zentralvergabestelle*, *ZVS* for short), foreigners may apply to individual universities of their choice. The *Akademische Auslandsamt* (advice bureau for foreign students) will help you. If the university administration proves intractable about some missing document, the *Auslandsamt* can often smooth the way.

Besides the equivalent of the *Reifezeugnis*, you will also need the following documents:
1. An insurance certificate. A certificate of insurance from the *AOK* (*Allgemeine Ortskrankenkasse*) today (1989) costs DM 62,25 and this ensures medical care under the *AOK* health scheme. There is no way round this unless your parents are already insured with a local health scheme that usually allows children to be included. Foreign insurance is not recognised by the *AOK* or by a university. Above all it is not recognised by local doctors who will demand cash on the nail for treatment. Membership of the *AOK* entitles you to treatment free of charge and the doctor bills the *AOK* directly.
2. A free bill of health from your local medical officer (*Gesundheitsamt*). In the case of American citizens this includes an Aids test.
3. A letter from parents stating that they can provide financial

Tips for Students

support to cover the period of study. Or some such statement to this effect.
4. Proof of competence in the German language. This can be provided by the local *Goethe Institute* (equivalent of the British Council or America House) back home or an equivalent examination body. Most German universities provide their own courses to teach German (*Deutschkurse für Ausländer*), but they must be taken *before* matriculation.
5. A *Führungszeugnis*, which is a statement from the Registry in Berlin (and costs DM 10) that you do not have a criminal record. Foreigners used to be expected to obtain one from home but the British police do not issue such certificates.

All the above, and this is most important, goes in tandem with obtaining a residence permit (*Aufenthaltsgenehmigung*).

Documents needed for Matriculation and Residence Permit

Matriculation:
University invitation (letter)
Insurance certificate (*AOK*)
Letter from parents for
financial support
(*Amtsärztliches Zeugnis*)
Medical certificate
Führungszeugnis

Residence Permit:
Passport
Photo
+ same documents as for
matriculation

Residence Permit

A residence permit to study will only be granted when a potential student has matriculated. Someone attending a language course before matriculation will only be given a provisional residence permit. Matriculation and obtaining the *Aufenthaltsgenehmigung* are interdependent.

The key to matriculating and to obtaining the *Aufenthaltsgenehmigung* is to have the necessary documents required for both operations. If any particular document is missing, both procedures can be held up. It is not just the delay that is so time consuming, but the time involved in walking or driving from one office to another, with each office being open only in the morning and, of course, closing at weekends and public holidays. Furthermore other people may be in the same position so considerable

Tips for Students

time is spent in queuing. It can be an enormous test of one's patience. The officials concerned, though friendly enough, are usually trying to get through an immense volume of paperwork and thus try to arrange things to serve their convenience rather than yours. Therefore, before visiting the different offices work out a strategy.

Remember the dual aim: matriculation and residence permit. Make sure you have all the documents for both, listed above. Then get a local map and mark where the University Registry is — this should be easy — the *Ordnungsamt* (Aliens Department) usually in the town hall (*Rathaus*), or at the main police station (*Polizeipräsidium*), the *AOK* and the *Gesundheitsamt*. Check to see when the relevant departments are open – there may be one day in the week when they are closed or open longer. Then work out how to get there. Take into consideration that one or more visits may be necessary. You may be in a hurry, but the office you are calling on won't be. Do not forget public holidays! There are many of them, especially in Southern Germany. Remember, too, that the official you are dealing with and who has been particularly helpful, may suddenly fall ill or may just take a day or two off. If negotiations have reached a tricky stage and the official has put your papers away, it does not necessarily mean that a colleague can find them. You may well be told to come back when the friendly official is there. Don't get exasperated, or at least too exasperated, because most people are that already and, of course, the official has the whip hand. Even if you bully him to accept one document in lieu of another, he can always ask for a new one. Play it cool and never try to make a joke of it. Bureaucracy in any form is taken extremely seriously in Germany. Remember that a third of the working population depend upon it for work.

BAFöG

In 1987 21 per cent of German students received grants (*BAFöG*) to help or wholly finance their studies. It is awarded according to a means test based on parental income. The highest sum payable if all conditions are met is DM 815 monthly. This sum is increased for study abroad. From 1990 onwards students will have to pay back only half of their grant instead of the whole lot.

Whilst many students feel that the *BAFöG (Bundesausbildungsförderungsgesetz)* they receive is insufficient, others

Tips for Students

recognise that without it they would not be able to study at all. However this only applies to German nationals.

Funding study in Germany: grants for foreign students
Studying in Germany is not cheap. Although there are no tuition fees to pay, you have to live. If you are doing a university sandwich course at home and a year in Germany to learn or polish up the language is a requirement of the course, then probably your university will have an agreement with a German university. In the UK, Aston and Leeds have agreements with Bayreuth University; in the USA, South Carolina and George Washington with Bamberg University. This is to mention only a few; there are many other such arrangements.

Student insurance
Vacation employment is an important consideration to be taken into account in connection with insurance. Additional insurance is not required if a student works less than 20 hours a week, or for not more than two months at a time, or for longer than the summer vacation, which is when most students take temporary employment. If these conditions are not fulfilled, then full insurance cover is required. There are exceptions to the conditions mentioned above – the 20 hours a week may be exceeded, for example, at the weekend or nights, if it can be established that a student's main occupation is studying. Another example occurs during the two months' vacation work period which itself may not exceed fifty calendar days (*Kalendertage*). If the work period exceeds two months other than during the vacation, then normal insurance is required from the third month on. This insurance, however, only begins after the exempted time has elapsed. More insurance is required if the student works for a total of twenty six weeks in the year and more than 20 hours per week. Make sure you observe the regulations because if you don't and you have a serious accident not only will you *not* receive compensation but your studies are interrupted too. If you work for longer periods than the *versicherungsfreie* period – that is, for more than two months in the vacations and for more than 20 hours a week in term time – then normal insurance must be paid for the whole period.

Students who complete their courses at a university may

Tips for Students

have this time recognised for up to five years as a period for which they do not have to contribute towards the State pension scheme (*Ausfallziet*). Should you decide to remain in Germany after graduation, this becomes important later on when it comes to calculating the pension due and the requisite period for which contributions were payable.

Difficulties experienced by German students
Finding a place at the university of your choice is a complicated business for German students. As explained, it is arranged by the *ZVS* (*Zentralvergabestelle*) in Darmstadt. Students are expected to attend the university nearest to their homes. A student from North Rhine Westphalia who wishes to attend Munich University may find this impossible. Educational standards are held to differ between North Rhine Westphalia and Bavaria and so an *Abitur* from the former *Land* is not considered as good as one from the latter. But even if the student wants to attend a Bavarian university, he or she may well have to accept a place at a provincial one instead.

Living expenses
Students can live in hostels (*Studentwohnheime*) or privately, either in digs, sharing a flat or even singly. Hostel accommodation may consist of single flatlets with cooking stove, shower with WC, with light and central heating included (rent varies from DM 140 to 280 in a large city like Munich, to DM 145 to 222 in a small town like Bayreuth), or single rooms sharing common facilities; some hostels have 4-bedroom flats that share facilities. Often there is a 'phone connection (*Telefonanschluß*) to each room so a phone contract will be drawn up with the local post office. The current charge for obtaining a telephone is DM 65, the standing monthly charge is DM 27, and Pf 23 is the charge per unit.

Generally there is a great shortage of student accommodation, both hostel and private. Foreign students will not find it any easier though some universities give priority to foreigners.

Accommodation is one thing, general living expenses for food, clothes and entertainment another. The rate of inflation is low in Germany (3.2 per cent in 1989), but the standard of living is high, and so are prices. For a foreign student living on an

Tips for Students

allowance or scholarship from home, exchange rates are vital, though at present rates *vis-à-vis* the DM are fairly constant. A friendly bank will help you obtain the best rate of exchange — see *Banks*, p62.

Exams

The German system relies upon the written word and also very strongly upon oral exams (*viva voces*). Whilst candidates for the written examinations are given a number so that their answer sheets remain anonymous, they may well be able to choose their examiner(s) for the viva. The reason for the latter is that a candidate should, where necessary, have the opportunity to discuss first with the examiner roughly what the examination is to be about. The theory is that the examiner should not seek to discover what the student does not know but how much he does know about a particular subject. And the mark is given accordingly. A candidate should be allowed to be examined by someone he knows, whose seminars he has attended or lectures he has listened to. On the whole the system works well enough so long as the examiner is not overloaded through overcrowding at his own university. Otherwise, as I have found in examining a horde of students, the poor examiner is overwhelmed and undoubtedly, however hard he tries, it is the candidate who suffers. A candidate who receives a poor mark may complain on technical grounds that the examination was unfairly conducted. The complaint has to be in writing and follows a special procedure; if it is upheld, the examination must be repeated, putting additional pressure on the examiner. Sometimes, however, complaints are ridiculous, such as the time a student complained that his examiner's clock was too loud! Students have told me that if they fail to get a good mark, they have nothing to lose by complaining on the off-chance that they may be able to improve their mark. They fail to take into consideration the very considerable waste of time caused to members of staff.

Exams: cheating

At one university in the English department the professors used to tell students well in advance the subjects on which they would be asked to write essays so that they could learn the answers by heart. A former English *Lektor* (lecturer) told me how absurd he and his colleagues felt as native speakers having to correct essays that were far better written than theirs would have been! *Never* hesitate to ask a member of staff if you have a question or are in difficulty with your studies. Every member of staff holds the celebrated *Sprechstunde* (counselling hour). If you want to consult a professor, it is customary to make an appointment to see him or her during the *Sprechstunde*. You are given a time to attend and thus at a large university do not have to wait so long (though it could be very long depending upon the standing of the professor concerned).

If you find it daunting talking to a professor in German, prepare what you are going to say beforehand. This gives you greater confidence and fluency. Don't expect the professor to be all smiles. It could be quite the reverse, but this is not your fault; you never know how much the student before may have irritated him.

Remember, above all else, that although professors have lost some of their power, they still have a lot left, not only over students but also over their assistants (*Assistenten*) who depend upon them for their future academic careers.

Now for more background information in detail which, as a student, you should find helpful in understanding what initially appears strange and totally unlike behaviour in an English-speaking university:

Doing colleagues favours – translations
Foreign academics on secondment or working at German universities should be exceedingly chary of taking on additional work as a favour outside the official duties, as laid down in the contract. In time the favour may become a burden which it is impossible to lay down and may well interfere with carrying out your official duties. Considerable tact, imagination and courage are required to say 'No', but it is better to do this at the beginning rather than regret it when it is too late. In any case a German professor worth his salt will understand the position. He will have been in the business long enough. A decent professor will offer to pay privately for correction or translating services, but even then do not accept this offer unless you have time to do the extra work involved. Remember that you have been contracted to do a special job, that you are being paid for this and this alone

Tips for Students

and if you do not get it done it may affect your whole future academic career. People are always available who can do translation work for a fee, but doubtless there are few able to do your job. I can only repeat: you have been warned. Stick to the contract. If you don't understand it, get someone who does to explain it to you; if there is any difficulty with your professor, show it to him. I have always found that when dealing with Germans, they respect you more for being firm — in a polite way — rather than being weak. Forget being a so-called English gentleman. It works only marginally in Germany. In the academic world, colleagues can be ruthless.

None of this holds if the person asking the favour is a personal friend as opposed to being a colleague. But the friend would usually not do this in the first place. Be careful too, of the professor who expects you to do translation or other editorial work without according you full published recognition. He or she may be reluctant to admit that your help was necessary or simply dislike sharing space on the title page with lowly you. Insist on a contract. Seek specialist legal advice on copyright and intellectual property. If you are a writer, join the *Gesellschaft* (society) *WORT* to ensure that you receive royalties (*Tantiemen*). Don't let others pick your brains for nothing!

German scholarship

German scholarship is unbeatable in its profundity, objectivity and achievements. It is an institution. Right from the specialisation course (*Leistungskurs* — see p37) and through university, pupils and then students learn how to write scholarly papers (*Seminararbeiten*) based on original research with primary and then secondary material. None of the superficial Oxbridge weekly essays or MAs without having to write a thesis. Accordingly, anyone who has been to grammar school and graduated from university at least knows how to begin to write in a scholarly fashion.

The special course (*Leistungskurs*) at grammar school involves writing a paper (*Facharbeit*), and the term seminar papers that undergraduate students are expected to write are each between twenty and thirty pages and require considerable application. From the papers *in English* handed in by my own students, writing in what for them is a foreign language, I can

Tips for Students

testify to the excellence of many. The German penchant for taking some things to extremes also helps to produce this excellence.

The resulting problems for students who do not turn in reasonable papers can be traumatic. The award of a poor mark may affect the student's future career at university, for example, whether or not the professor invites a student to write a thesis and perhaps become his assistant.

It might mean that the whole semester's work (which means six months because there are usually only two terms ie, *Semester*, a year) has been for nothing. A particular seminar may be held only once a year and so a student must wait a whole year to repeat it and thus holds up his whole course of studies. This is the personal side of the coin.

The other, public, one is the continued pursuit of excellence. Young people learn to write, work and think in a scholarly way. Those who continue at university, write a dissertation and then, having served their stint as a professor's assistant, write a *Habilitation* (unknown in English-speaking academe), which is a superior, longer kind of dissertation: these are scholars indeed. The fact that few people, except colleagues, will ever read the tomes they write (and indeed, if so disposed, would ever understand what they read) is beside the point. For the academic it is 'publish or perish'. Scholarship and research remain on separate levels, in the humanities as opposed to the natural sciences, not always of much use to anybody and costing the taxpayer millions.

Academe is under strain at present because of a shortage of posts. It is also becoming increasingly difficult for scholars to publish books without government assistance. Many scholarly works are just glorified vanity publications of little interest to general readers. The other problem for German academics is that few foreigners read German, so much of it must be translated into English if it is to be read at all outside German-speaking countries — see *Doing colleagues favours*, p137. In any case German natural scientists write in English, otherwise they would have little chance of making an impact abroad. It is, of course, a scientific English that an English-speaking layman would find difficult to understand, but it serves its purpose and is really a world language.

German scholarship is thus based on a thorough training

and is pursued with great dedication. If you want to know in detail about a subject there is usually a German scholar who has worked on it and even if out-of-date his work will provide something solid to start with. But it won't necessarily be elegantly phrased, or a pleasure to read. The gentleman scholar, the gifted amateur, has always appeared far less frequently in Germany than in English-speaking countries. German scholarship has nearly always been professional.

Academe

The Germans' inordinate respect for learning is explicit in the high social position accorded university teachers (see *Social attitudes — titles*, p93) and recognition that hitherto a good education was passport to a good job and thus a meal ticket for life. On the latter score disillusion has set in because of the high number of unemployed graduates. Furthermore education is very costly, the period of study longer than in English-speaking countries and, depending upon the *Länder* in question (education being a preserve of the *Länder* as opposed to the Federal Government the *Bund*), there is an acute shortage of money to maintain existing universities as well as to continue with the building of those under construction. Unlike the United States, there are no private universities; most universities are run by the State, and a few by the Church. One 'distance-learning' university (the University of Hagen) gives correspondence courses and uses video-cassettes, and although much smaller, approximates to the English Open University. The private university of Flensburg has just gone bankrupt (1989).

A President or Rector and a Registrar have key positions in universities, which are run by an administration (*Verwaltung*) that in turn is controlled by the local Ministry of Science and Research. The senior professor, with a chair (*Lehrstuhl*), rules supreme within the different faculties. There are several ranks of professor:

C4 at the top, with a staff of assistants (*Assistenten*), a secretary and, depending upon his or her discipline, a large or modest number of students to teach; then C3 and C2 professors (*außerordentlicher Professor*), approximating to American assistant professors and British senior lecturers respectively, who do not enjoy the status of the senior C4 (*Lehrstuhlinhaber*). A

Tips for Students

professor is an official and therefore unsackable (*unkündbar*). Other university teachers, who are *Beamter*, also have tenure. There are also *Privatdozenten*, that is those who are qualified to become a professor but have not yet been appointed to a chair.

How does one become a professor? A bright student who has done well in the final examinations might be invited by his professor to become his assistant (*Assistent*), whilst writing a doctorate (*Doktorarbeit*), the professor being his supervisor (*Doktorvater*). This enables the assistant to draw a salary whilst writing his thesis. Someone who writes a doctorate is called a *Doktorand* but does not have to become an *Assistent*. However, the *Assistent* is usually required to teach four hours a week and also help his professor both in correcting papers and with administration. He is completely dependent upon the professor — some say he is the latter's 'slave'! If his dissertation is to the professor's liking and satisfies the faculty, all is well. He has his doctorate and may continue with the same professor, providing a post (*Planstelle*) is available for him. If not, he will have to try for another position at the university so that he can write his *Habilitation* whilst receiving a salary. The *Habilitation* (*Habil* for short — see p139) is a mega-dissertation that must be defended as a whole, or in part, in person before the faculty. When all the formal requirements are complete (which may include a period of teaching at the university for an extra period before fulfilling a regulation period), the candidate then awaits the invitation (*Ruf*) for a professorship.

One can wait for ever, like a politician awaiting the call from the Prime Minister's secretary to be made minister. Briefly, to get the *Ruf*, both *Privatdozenten* and professors wishing to change universities must answer advertisements in the appointments' columns of the press to submit themselves for selection. A shortlist is made and relevant candidates invited to give a lecture (called as a joke *Vorsingen*: 'singing in front of others') and answer questions from members of the selection board of the faculty. From this shortlist an even shorter shortlist of three candidates will be submitted to the local Ministry of Science and Research in order of preference. The minister then chooses a candidate and it may well be the last name on the list.

The *Ruf* is then sent to the successful candidate and negotiations begin. If the candidate is already a professor at another university he may well also negotiate with his own university and ministry to see if he can improve his salary and facilities to such an extent that the new chair at the other university no longer appears so attractive. Indeed this may have been the professor's tactic all along. Or it could be that he genuinely wants to move but his own university wants to keep him. Negotiations can last a long time and in the end prove abortive. In this case, the second name on the list may be offered the post or the whole procedure may have to be repeated because the university does not want to have either of the other candidates. The masculine pronoun has been used throughout because there are so few female professors.

All this aims to be very fair and objective but is sometimes the reverse, especially if the university and the ministry disagree on an appointment. It has been known for a ministry to force a candidate upon a university, for the latter to go to court on the matter, lose the case, be forced to accept the ministry's choice and then for the faculty concerned to send the new professor to Coventry. In one case the professor died a few years later and another professor, from a different university, commented, 'They killed him'. No doubt C.P. Snow would have found great material for a German university novel!

Universities in retrospect: the sixties
As in other European countries, students protested in the sixties with great bravado. In Germany they undoubtedly had a case as far as the autocratic way some professors ruled their roosts. The university professor used to be all-powerful. He has always been what the German call a *Respektperson* (someone to be looked up to) and save during the Nazi régime when everybody was made to toe the line, he reigned supreme because so many — student and assistant — depended on him; students for their marks during term and in finals, assistants for their jobs. The result was that some professors, often overworked with increasing numbers of students, abused their power and the system being what it was, there was little anyone could do about it.

The students had their own organisation ASTA (*Allgemeiner Studentenausschuß*) which became highly politicised, left-wing and militant. Notorious students such as Fritz Teufel and Helmut Pohl (both served terms or are still serving terms of

Tips for Students

imprisonment) often took control. Groups of militants visited lectures and seminars trying to force professor and student alike to discuss topics such as the *Notstandsgesetzbebung* (State of Emergency Laws) or the death of student demonstrator Benno Ohnesorge in Berlin during the late Shah's visit there. If the professor and students refused, the militant group broke up the lecture. Some professors were able to resist, some not; studies suffered. I remember such scenes vividly when my own professor was shouted down in class and in the lecture hall. Things escalated. The locks to professors' office doors were filled with glue; graffiti were scrawled everywhere. Students also took to the streets and battles ensued, with the police ill-trained for such a task.

One thing the universities did *not* do was call in the police, except in Munich where students successfully prevented the installation of the new university president; the Bavarian State arranged for the ceremony to be held in the *Residenz* (former royal palace) under police protection. That was in the time of Rudi Dutschke (who was ultimately shot in the head, from which he only partially recovered and then subsequently died) and Daniel Cohn-Bendit, who has now become a member of the Frankfurt City Council.

As far as the general public was concerned, many people who had not been privileged to attend university felt that students had gone too far; that they should get down to their studies and make use of the very expensive facilities put at their disposal and paid for by the taxpayer.

There is a legacy from those days: student's demands are taken seriously even if they are not always met. Students in turn are now mainly determined to get a job as soon as they can. They demand efficiently run courses. This can only be for the good of all.

The student revolt of the sixties was not a class war, although students wanted to change society (*Gesellschaft*); many student leaders were middle class, coming from most respectable homes. A later Bavarian Minister of Education, Hans Maier, said that looking back, it was 'an attempt by students at revolution by taking over lecture halls'. Their problem was that the lecture hall was not society, nor was the university the State. The country could get on quite well without students and in time the latter

Tips for Students

realised that ultimately they needed jobs and, for this, exams and a return to studies were necessary.

The State and the *Länder* had learnt their lesson. Some of the *Länder* banned *ASTA* (the student union) and all restructured the universities, stripping the professors of some power by grouping the different chairs (*Lehrstühle*) together in *Fachbereiche* instead of individual faculties (*Fakultäten*). The latter were now controlled by a council (*Fachbereichsrat*) under the chairmanship of the dean supported by representatives of the professors, assistants, students and administrative staff, but so weighted in numbers as to still give the professors an over-all majority.

In the conservative (*CDU/CSU*) *Länder*, students from different faculties were allowed to elect representatives called *Fachschaftssprecher* (council speakers) to special student councils (*Fachschaften*). Student groups still elected members to the *Fachschaft*, but the *Fachschaft*, as a whole, though it might favour one particular political direction, was not itself allowed to assume the power and influence possessed by the old *ASTA* in the past.

Elsewhere *ASTA* continued, but nowadays funds must be used for purely student activities, which now follow more pragmatic lines; students agitate for improved conditions and better facilities rather than for worldwide political causes.

In fact all that students in the sixties achieved was the appearance and some substance of democracy, stripping professors of some of their power but ensuring, in the main, an increase in the power of ministries and the civil service. Today's students, however, are more concerned with getting a job than with changing society or the world.

The problems in universities today

By tradition, the German university derives much from Wilhelm von Humboldt (1766–1835) a celebrated scholar and luminary who was a Prussian official in the Education Ministry for a few months in 1809. Whilst being somewhat obscure, and therefore often unintelligible, his pronouncements have nonetheless been treated with great respect by succeeding generations even though few have read them in context. He believed firmly in a combination of research and teaching (*Forschung und Lehre*) where students actually participate in research, not as in those countries where research as such is for academics only, and universities are mainly for getting students through exams.

No one knows what Humboldt would have made of the present situation where, in 1987, 1,360,000 students (ten times as many as in 1952) were enrolled at university; and, what is more important, where there are simply not enough jobs for graduates. The problem is that nowadays with such a shortage of jobs and the age at which students complete their studies (sometimes 28+ or with a doctorate 31+), purely academic research is becoming increasingly regarded as a luxury.

Law studies at universities do not prepare students to pass the State law exams (first *Referendarexamen*) because the teaching syllabus is based too much on theory, also would-be lawyers learn little that will be of practical use when they ultimately practise law. As it is, law students generally attend crammers (*Repetitorien*) to get through the exams. Unless they intend to become academics themselves, students regard law courses at university as an excellent mental exercise but, in practical terms, an expensive waste of time. Future clients want a lawyer who can either win cases or help in practical ways to further their business. Usually those with the best marks in the exams elect to work for the State, either as judges or in ministries of the Federal Government or the *Länder*. There they find too that what they have absorbed at university is of little direct use.

Some academics claim that law courses and the books colleagues now write are becoming diluted; that pure scholarship (law is regarded as a science — *Rechtswissenschaft*) is being usurped by examination requirements.

Humboldt would have been particularly perturbed by the overcrowding that has now become part and parcel of study at university. Lecture halls are overfilled, so that lectures have to be relayed outside by video; considerable delays occur while professors or their assistants correct papers and theses, and students are frustrated to such a degree that they end up boycotting lectures, going on strike and disrupting inner city traffic with protest marches. Nobody is satisfied; neither staff nor students. The result is the imposition of a *numerus clausus* (restricted entry) for some university subjects against the will

Tips for Students

of local ministries of science and art (*Wissenschaft und Kunst*). Both parties then appeal to the courts.

Much of the problem could be solved by streamlining both the grammar schools (*Gymnasien*) and university courses and by channelling off subjects such as business studies either to special academies or to business schools or technical colleges and polytechnics (*Fachhochschulen*) where essentially pragmatically minded students would be spared the elaborate procedure of university which they really do not appreciate.

The real problem today is how to make education cost effective, without ruining it, and relevant to the needs of modern society. As the Federal Constitution guarantees every student with 'A' level *Abitur* (*Reifezeugnis*) a place at university, assuming the number of staff is not increased and that students numbers increase, the system will become even more overloaded than it is already. It was thought that the fall in the birthrate would ease matters but what was not foreseen was the rise in unemployment.

German language qualifications

On paper German language requirements are very strict. One is expected to pass this and that exam. Whilst no doubt true in most cases, some foreign students whose knowledge of German is fairly basic nonetheless slip through the net. This is not an invitation to follow suit but an encouragement not to give up if you find it difficult to learn the language quickly. Some very intelligent people experience difficulty with foreign languages because they are not especially sociable, perhaps even slightly introverted. You learn languages only when you speak them! Those who find it especially difficult at first may lack fluency when they do speak, but make few mistakes, and in time are able to write reasonably well. Be patient and don't give up if you find the language difficult. When you reach university, if you find writing a *Seminararbeit* (paper) overwhelming, some kind German student will usually help you. German students can be very kind, as are the staff.

15
Understanding Current Events

Behind the News
If you turn on the television and watch the news at 8 or 10 pm, it is useful to know something of the background to the West German constitution and politics.

West Germany has a Federal and a written constitution inaugurated in 1949. The President as Head of State is elected by members of the *Bundestag*, that is the lower house, which is responsible for suggesting, initiating, considering and passing legislation, much of which also has to be approved by the second chamber, the *Bundesrat*. Members are elected to the *Bundestag* by universal suffrage, that is, all those aged 18 and over, according to a system of proportional representation. Each voter has two votes: one for the local candidate in his *Wahlkreis* (constituency), the other for the list of candidates selected by the different parties. The votes for the lists (*Listenwahl*) are awarded to parties proportionate to the total votes awarded each list. Thus, unlike the British Parliament, although a party may not win many seats directly it will nonetheless be represented. In order to avoid a number of small so-called '*Splitterparteien*' as in the Weimar Republic, unless a party obtains at least 5 per cent of the votes cast it is not awarded a percentage of seats.

The *Bundesrat* is composed of representatives from the *Länder* — each of the *Länder* has at least three votes — according to their population; thus Bavaria, one of the larger *Länder*, has five representatives, Hessen four, and one of the smaller states, Bremen, three. The *Bundesrat* was intended as a restraining influence on the *Bundestag* and on average has to approve over half the legislation passed by the latter. In the case of disagreement, there is a procedure of mediation which, when exhausted, results in the *Bundestag* winning the day, though this usually occurs only after substantial concessions have been made by the lower house.

The *Bundespräsident* (Federal President) finally has to approve legislation before it is enacted. He can withhold his consent if he thinks that it is unconstitutional. He refers the matter to the Federal Constitutional Court (*Bundesverfassungsgericht*) which decides one way or the other. The majority of members of the *Bundestag* are officials (*Beamten*) and male, and Federal Chancellor Helmut Kohl has said that it is the Achilles' heel of German democracy that not more women are elected. It is also regrettable that membership of the *Bundestag* is not more representative of the population.

The Federal President is largely a ceremonial figure, but can assume a certain importance when he is a person of stature. Presidents Heuß and von Weizsäcker showed stature and imagination in office though the latter, whilst highly respected, took some initiatives that were not appreciated by certain sections of the public eg, when he pardoned a former terrorist serving a prison sentence. In general the Federal Chancellor rules the roost, chooses Federal ministers and members of the Cabinet.

Democracy

The government of the day is headed by the Federal Chancellor (*Bundeskanzler*) who may be, but is not always, chairman of his own political party. He selects the ministers for appointment by the Federal President. The main parties are CDU (*Christliche Demokratische Union*), Christian Democratic Union — which is an alliance with the Bavarian *CSU* (*Christliche Soziale Union*), Christian Social Union — together in a government coalition with the *FDP* (*Freie Demokratische Partei*) Free Democratic Party: the Liberals. The Liberals formed a coalition government with the *SPD* (*Sozialdemokratische Partei Deutschland*) Social Democratic Party of Germany (1969–1982). The Liberals, who in some of the *Länder* parliaments barely command 5 per cent of the votes cast, are referred to as the '*Zünglein an der Waage*' (tipping the scales) because they enjoy power disproportionate to the number of votes.

The Federal Constitution is designed to avoid the mistakes and weaknesses of the Weimar Republic without allowing a repetition of the Third Reich. Government must be strong enough to survive anti-democratic forces but not too strong to avoid democratic control. It is a case of trying to achieve the right framework of checks and balances.

Understanding Current Events

Proportional representation has allowed the limited resurgence of right-wing parties, such as the *NPD* (*Nationaldemokratische Partei Deutschland*) — National Democratic Party of Germany — which is associated in some people's minds with the Nazis, though the NPD would strenuously deny this. There is a party, semi-outlawed, which definitely was Nazi, with members wearing uniforms, doing drill and military training. This was stopped; the people were arrested and put on trial. The official Communist Party is very small but one feels its influence is, or can be at times, very great. The extent to which it receives assistance from East Germany is unclear.

Danger to democracy lies not only from the extreme right but also from the extreme left. Until 1965 the Communist Party (*Kommunistische Partei Deutschland*) was banned but the *Deutsche Kommunistische Partei* was legalised in 1968. It seemed less dangerous to allow it to operate openly rather than to force it to work in secret. And time has shown this to be the wiser course, because the Communists win so few votes at elections.

Where government is less tolerant is at local *Länder* level. As already stated, West Germany has a Federal Constitution and government. However, each of the *Länder* has its own government with a *Ministerpräsident* (Prime Minister and Chief representative of the *Land*) with a cabinet, parliament (*Landtag*) and in Bavaria, a second chamber (*Senat*). The *Länder* decide on matters of justice, including the police, education, energy, environment and agriculture though there are also Federal ministries of justice, research and the environment.

Again the idea is that the Federal Government should not have too much power *vis-à-vis* the governments of the *Länder* so that it would be difficult for one man to take over again. Whilst foreign relations and defence, together with the Border police (*Bundesgrenzschutz*) are in the hands of the Federal Government, a powerful and influential *Land* leader like the late Bavarian *Ministerpräsident* Franz Joseph Strauß can make his own foreign policy. In any case the Bavarians are renowned for being different and acting independently. Strauß virtually ignored the Federal Foreign Minister Hans Dietrich Genscher in his celebrated journey to Moscow and his much criticised visit to

South and South-West Africa. Bavaria has its own ambassador to the Holy See.

It is significant how many national organisations there are and the important role they play in the nation's affairs, though ultimately they depend upon the Federal Government for funds to underwrite their proposals. To sum up, whilst Bonn decides most things, the *Länder* have a definite say, especially in local matters. Sometimes this has national significance as with the problem of loyalty to the constitution, and the democratic form of government in which Communist Party members have no share. All this was taken very seriously by conservative governments, such as in Bavaria, where civil servants were dismissed for being members of the party. Their *Verfassungstreue* (loyalty to the constitution) was considered suspect.

However, this raises the question of the freedom to work and the choice of political opinion, rights guaranteed by the constitution. Some of the *Länder* consider that where a citizen's individual rights are preserved at the cost of the Constitution itself, the Constitution takes priority.

Foreigners do not have the right to vote in general elections but there is a move to allow them to vote in elections at municipal level because it is recognised and accepted that they are members of the community.

Politics rarely affect the foreign visitor at first. Political parties seem to concern themselves with essentially local problems. Eventually you become involved when legislation affects labour laws, the hours to be worked each week — 38½ — before overtime is payable, income tax, and other matters that do concern you.

Those interested in environmental issues will be concerned with attempts made by government and local authorities to contain acid rain by reducing toxic emissions. The imposition of a speed limit on the motorways, disposal of toxic waste in rivers, purity of the air, affect the lives of all who live in Germany. Questions of arms control in a country bordering the Iron Curtain are of interest, too.

Asylverfahren

One problem that has had a profound effect upon German politics is connected with foreigners — the refugee problem. Not

Understanding Current Events

only does the Constitution encourage refugees to seek asylum in Germany but the appeals procedure in the courts, should application for asylum be refused, can prevent expulsion for years. Enquiries must be made in the refugee's homeland, translators have to be available and various other delaying tactics can be employed. Moreover, whilst the refugee is going through this procedure he or she, if young enough and single, might well marry a German or form an attachment and have a child born in Germany and thus automatically obtain citizenship.

Recent concern about the influx of refugees has had a profoundly worrying effect upon German politics; adherents to the middle of the road who eschew the extreme left or right have lost support, as recent local election results show. People see themselves and the secure lives they lead being swamped by those willing to work for less money — see *Society*, p87 — increasing the demand for accommodation and social facilities (health care, education, insurance and so on) while not always prepared to accept the German mores or way of life. Some Germans do not want to accept Turks as members of their own society and thus, by default, encourage them to stick together, thus exacerbating the problem. Germans see their hard-earned *Wirtschaftswunder* becoming a nightmare with so many unemployed. When they feel themselves being swamped, the only thing they can do about it is to protest by transferring their allegiance from the centre parties to the right-wing extremists.

This weakens the *CSU-CDU* coalition with the *FDP*, which itself is steadily losing support, and raises the question as to whether the *FDP* will have to change sides again and join the *SPD* in order to survive. In the meantime the Greens have increased in number, although this party is bitterly divided between the old fundamentalists devoted to saving the environment at any price, and the pragmatists who want power and are prepared to get it by joining either of the two larger political groups at *Länder* level.

The increase in support for the extreme right-wing frightens those left of centre into moving further left or merely joining the *Alternativen Parteien* (the Alternatives). The latter are small splinter groups who refuse to accept the traditional parties or their policies. Their loyalty to the Constitution, their observance or respect for law and order is sometimes in doubt. The same holds for significant elements among the Greens. It is difficult to generalise but it seems that some among the Greens and the Alternatives (and according to the *CDU* and the *CSU*, also among the *SPD*) do not wholeheartedly accept the traditional State, law and order etc; they sympathise with the *RAF* (*Republikanische Armee Fraktion*) terrorists while not believing themselves in violence or in using force to achieve their ends. They believe in democracy but have lost faith in the present political parties as a means of obtaining it.

It is true that many senior politicians have been taken to court accused of being involved in political scandals (*Affären*) but were then virtually let off — and the voters don't like that. However, as with Count Lambsdorf, their financial support is essential – obtaining contributions for party funds (the *Spendenaffäre*) is a very complicated question which has not yet been resolved satisfactorily. How can they be financed except by wealthy private contributions which are tax deductible? Yet if 'tax deductible' means payment for favours granted, the issue becomes extremely complicated in terms of political science.

The important thing is that many people have become very cynical about politics in general and certain politicians in particular. All this places great strains on German democracy which is still very young. There is always the danger that if enough people from the right or the left become disenchanted with the present system, they will try simpler, more extreme solutions, as in the past.

German democracy did withstand the student revolts of the sixties and has been sufficiently flexible to deal with *Haus-besetzungen* (squatting) in Hamburg, though in Berlin it was another matter. So far, so good, but the refugee problem remains a cause for concern — although this matter has caused concern in English-speaking and other European countries too. But still one asks: could it happen again?

Although Adolf Hitler was not an educated man, possibly a maniac, he certainly understood how to fire the dissatisfied, unemployed masses, manipulate the irresolute leaders of the Weimar Republic and exterminate opposition. His obsession with the Jews — his genocidal final solution to the 'problem' — was his downfall. An Austrian, he subjugated and demeaned Germany. Auschwitz and Belsen, Dachau and Ravensbruck can never be forgotten. Such atrocities are easier to judge than to understand. The extraordinary thing, however, about it all was, that so many of the inexplicably dastardly acts that occurred were either officially ordered or followed directly from official orders. Ordinary people (soldiers and prison guards) became animals. They no longer behaved like human beings.

It is this which was and is still so frightening. It is equally terrifying in all societies where individual rights are crushed by the alleged rights of the State. What baffles the English-speaking observer is that many of the officials responsible for such barbarities under Hitler argued that they were not responsible. They had merely acted under orders from above. What they did — one hears the phrase still — was merely a *Verwaltungsakt* (administrative act). I have to be honest and say that whilst I cannot imagine a recurrence of Nazi atrocities in the future, what goes on in East German political prisons is by all accounts not very pleasant. German officials are capable of callous behaviour and think nothing of it because they do not consider it their job to think. As officials they are there merely to carry out the directives of the State. As a mechanism in the wrong hands, this is obviously open to misuse, but there is a saving grace; lessons *have* been learnt from recent history.

Germany and abroad (foreign relations?)
The average German may be regional, even rural, but he is also interested in what goes on abroad. The coverage in German newspapers of events in English-speaking countries is far more comprehensive than vice versa. Some Americans in the mid-west are supposed not to know the difference between East and West Germany and, it is reported, think that a war is still going on in Germany!

Germany has been exposed to foreign influences because of the war and the continued existence of the military zones in Western and Eastern Germany. American films still predominate on television and the presence of large numbers of American soldiers influence everyday German life.

Germany also has a soft spot for the Third World and contributes generously to various projects there, especially in Africa. Such aid (*Entwicklungshilfe*) is usually linked with the furtherance of German business interests; it serves, too, to offset

Understanding Current Events

the extent of trade with South Africa. The present government refuses to join in sanctions against that country although certain — mainly military — products may not be exported there (but at times still are).

Germany's relationship with South Africa is complicated by the fact that South-West Africa belonged to the German Empire from 1884–1915. Many Germans still live there and some have emigrated to South Africa. Thus there are relations at a personal level.

The situation is still more complicated at national political level. Officially West Germany is against apartheid, but the *SCU*, under the late Franz Josef Strauß, was prepared to fraternise with the South African government – witness the visit undertaken by Strauß a few months before his death, much to the annoyance of the West German Foreign Minister, Hans Dietrich Genscher *FDP*, who complained that Strauß was trying to do his job for him.

The Federal Government has a thorny problem trying to keep on the right side of both the Israelies and the Arabs (the latter when it comes to dealing with terrorists), without offending the Americans. War-guilt still colours Germany's relations with Israel and though West Germany is forced to tread warily with the Arabs — West Germany has little oil — she does manage to steer a course that allows her to give substantial support to Israel without irking the Arabs too much. Of course, West Germany distinguishes between the different Arab factions and has had several hostages taken in the Lebanon. She has also had to deal with Arab terrorists operating within West Germany as well as having to cope with terrorists (eg Muhammed Ali Hamadei) wanted by the Americans and caught on arrival in the Federal Republic. Officially the Federal Government may not intervene in the judicial procedure of the *Länder* — justice being their preserve — or at least this can be used as an excuse for letting justice run its course when not meeting the demands for extradition of accused terrorists to the United States.

West Germany is in a very difficult position when it comes to dealing with the hi-jacking of its own aircraft and the passengers aboard. However, under Helmut Schmidt in October 1977, great decisiveness and skill were shown in freeing the German hostages in the *Lufthansa* plane held by terrorists in Mogadishu when a German team of special élite troops flew there and accomplished the rescue.

The European Community

West Germany is very much a member of the European Community. Such membership affects beer and sausage sales in the Federal Republic, allowing less stringent regulations as to the composition of the beverage or food to be imported and sold, contrary to local legislation — see *Eßkultur*, p167.

It also affects the treatment of, and working conditions for foreigners. Basically under the law a foreigner is equal with nationals but often without the residential status that would enable him to pursue a case in the local courts. This is in any case guaranteed by the German constitution. However no such equality exists in some areas of labour law, nor in certain professions such as in the treatment of teachers, in particular of *Lektoren* (lecturers), on short-term contracts who are nonetheless expected to work as though they had tenure. Such people have heavy teaching loads, as heavy or even heavier than their German colleagues who possess tenure. Many foreign teachers feel that they are treated as immigrant workers. However, a recent decision at the European Court at Luxembourg should help ease the lot of foreign teaching assistants. The subject is complicated and must be seen from the German point of view which is influenced by the very high rate of unemployment among teachers. Moreover, under local labour law, foreigners may appeal to the courts if they feel their rights have been disregarded. The cost of going to law is borne mainly by the unions which are very generous and supportive in this respect.

Defence

Apart from the involved subject of defence through NATO in answer to the threat from the East, most Germans are concerned with the relatively long period of National Service required of young men (not women) – 18 months, shortly to be extended to 2 years to compensate for the falling birth rate. Many people feel that this is too long. It is possible to be recognised as a conscientious objector but the procedure is not easy. If recognised as such, the young person must then do social service (*Zivildienst*) in old peoples' homes, hospitals etc.

Understanding Current Events

People living near military establishments are worried by the danger and high-level noise caused by low-level flying (*Tiefflüge*), which the military claim is necessary to provide adequate defence in time of war. Recently there have been several accidents with loss of civilian life which have caused people to wonder whether low-level flying, with its accident-prone pilots, is not more dangerous in the immediate future than any possible benefit which it might bring in the long-run.

Moreover, the noise causes disturbance and much irritation to the general public. Protests, petitions and public discussion have focussed attention on the subject and recently court judgements have forced the Ministry of Defence to cut down on low-level flying.

Church and religion

As in English-speaking countries church attendance is down except on high days and holidays. Both the Roman Catholic and the Protestant (*Evangelische Kirche*) churches have signed concordats with the respective governments of the *Länder* which regulate the relationship between Church and State.

The history of Church-State relations has not always been a happy one, particularly Bismarck's *Kulturkampf* (struggle) with the Pope. The concordat arrangement whereby the State arranges for the church to receive between 6 and 8 per cent of every person's taxable wage or salary gives both Catholic and Protestant churches great economic resources and influence.

Both churches run schools and charities. The Catholic welfare organisation called *Caritas* is very powerful, running hospitals, clinics and other welfare organisations. In all it is possibly the third largest employer in the country dealing – as does its Protestant sister organisation, *Diakonisches Werk der Evangelischen Kirche* – with all the social problems with which the State at national and local government level is unable to cope. The Catholic Church is more influential in the south and around Cologne (which used to belong to Bavaria) than in the north where the *Evangelische Kirche* is stronger.

What affects many Germans is the payment of church taxes — *Kirchensteuer*. For this a citizen has a right to be married and buried, his children baptized and confirmed in church. If a person belongs to the Church and decides to leave (*Austreten aus der Kirche*) he or she may do so and then be excused paying *Kirchensteuer*.

Foreigners who are not Catholics and not members of the *Evangelische Kirche* (the latter is unlikely) are not required to pay *Kirchensteuer*. Being a member of the Church of England is distinct and regarded as taxless.

Among certain sections of the population there is great opposition to the secular influence of the Church, whichever denomination, though in general it is the Catholic Church that excites the most opposition, because it is the stronger of the two.

In the south, church and politics go together. The *CSU* (Christian Social Union), the late Franz Josef Strauß's party, is closely allied to the Church. However the Bavarian Government is also careful to maintain good relations with the *Evangelische Kirche*.

What does, however, strike the foreigner visitor to Germany is the large number of public (ie, Church) holidays, especially in the Catholic south, which are gratefully observed by people of all and no denominations!

Unions

Officially the unions are non-political but in fact they are left-wing and thus unofficially allied with the *SPD* (Social Democratic Party). Generally they are prepared to do business with any government and any government with them. By being non-politically allied officially — dues cannot be automatically deducted from employees' pay packets nor do they give financial support to members of the *Bundestag* (as in the UK with trade union MPs) — they don't feel obliged necessarily to adopt intransigent positions. They are never prepared or determined to wreck the whole system, the economy, or, indeed, capitalism itself to achieve wage demands. Naturally there are political overtones but in general trade union leaders such as Franz Steinköhler of *IG Metall* (*Industriegewerkschaft Metall*), give more the impression of being senior business executives rather than politically inspired rabble rousers.

Fundamentally the German worker is too middle class to want to risk everything for a long pointless strike that would eat up his savings and put his mortgage at risk. The union knows this and tries to avoid massive strikes, preferring selective ones at key factories or points in the chain of production or supply. The employers then answer with a general lock-out. Lock-outs are legal under German labour law but where employees are willing to work but are prevented from doing so as in the case of a lock-out, questions arise as to whether they could apply for social assistance. It was decided that workers who were locked out could not claim assistance but those in secondary factories or firms who as a result of the lock-out were left without work could. Thus there is a lock-out in Company A (those workers may not claim social assistance) which throws workers in Company B out of work who may claim assistance so long as they do not belong to the same trade union or group of workers involved in the original strike.

Under the present system if a worker goes on strike neither he nor his family is entitled to social assistance because he is held responsible for the welfare of himself and his family. Legislation was introduced by the present *CDU, CSU-FDP* government prohibiting social assistance for workers who were locked out.

Unemployment

Unemployment is uncomfortably high at near 2 million and further pressures are added through the influx of *Aussiedler* and *Heimkehrer* and *Wirtschaftsflüchtlinge*. Additionally, the pressure by the trade unions to reduce weekly working hours from (1989) 37½ to 35, whilst ostensibly aimed at forcing employers to increase the labour force, may achieve the opposite in the long-run by forcing employers to invest in more automation and so increase unemployment. Employers only take on more labour when increased demand for their products warrants doing so. Unless labour becomes more productive when it becomes more expensive, it becomes less competitive at home and abroad and the problem of unemployment is exacerbated and not alleviated.

One can appreciate though, how workers feel solidarity with unemployed colleagues and those others recently thrown out of work. While there is nearly always work for qualified labour, the semi-skilled or unskilled worker (for example, in the rationalised steel or shrinking coal industry) finds it virtually impossible to retrain or to obtain new employment.

What complicates the issue of unemployment still further is

the unions' determination to resist weekend work. Employers who have invested in expensive machinery claim that such an attitude is inflexible and designed to make their products too expensive on the world market. A recent strike won printers an official reduction in Saturday work for the first time; it was not accepted by Gruner & Jahr, one of the major publishing and printing houses, which left the Publishers' Association to underline its point, and will lead other publishers to have printing work done in Italy and other, cheaper, places.

The whole question of unemployment is not just a political but a social problem. Unions committed to resisting weekend work in order to reduce working hours, are adopting a stance, recognised by reform-socialists like Oscar Lafontaine (*Ministerpräsident* of Saarland) as being totally out of date. The real struggle within the labour movement is how to find a compromise between the dictates of class struggle and the realities of a modern economy – and this concerns the question of longer opening hours.

Experiments are being made with a late opening night for shops in some cities. The unions resist this because they are afraid that employees could be required to work unsocial hours without overtime. The idea of having supermarkets and the like open 24 hours a day, as in America, is as yet considered revolutionary.

Moonlighting

According to the President of the Federal Department for Work (*Bundesanstalt für Arbeit*), Dr Heinrich Franke, moonlighting (*Schwarzarbeit*) amounted to between 5 and 10 per cent of the social product in 1989 – that is, 110 to 220 milliard Marks per annum. Moreover, Franke estimates that this costs 100,000 to 50,000 jobs *and* it costs the State insurance and accident schemes a considerable amount of money in lost contributions from employers and employees.

Moonlighting assumes various forms — manual workers using in their free-time the skills for which they are normally paid at work, but charging less to the customer; those on unemployment benefit working without declaring it; employers and employees conspiring to incorporate non-existent, so-called ghost workers so that one man's work is shared with several imaginary people who, because they only work part-time, do

Understanding Current Events

not pay insurance contributions etc; and worst of all, the so-called *Verleiher* (labour contractors) who 'lend out' workers, often foreigners without work permits who will work for lower wages than they should receive, to employers who claim that they are only using the workers on loan and not employing them directly. The employers thus get cheap labour for which insurance contributions are rarely paid. A special social identity card (*Sozialausweis*) is to be introduced which workers will be required to produce on demand to prove that their contributions are being paid.

It would be an over-simplification to blame the 'employers' or 'hirers' of labour. In agriculture where seasonal labour is employed and has to be employed quickly (for example, to harvest fruit), the only feasible source of labour available is from Third World immigrants, who do an excellent job but wish to remain anonymous, leaving all negotiations to the labour contractor. An employer who tries to avoid working with the contractor is doomed to failure because suitable local labour is not available.

Gastarbeiter

Undoubtedly sometimes *Gastarbeiter* are exploited by unscrupulous or insensitive employers seeking cheap labour to do dirty jobs that local workers would not do. A highly publicised report by a writer, Günter Wallraff, drew attention recently to some of the worst abuses, some committed by large, well-known companies, which hired immigrant labour to do dirty jobs through labour contractors. Wallraff pretended to be a *Gastarbeiter* to see what went on in some companies and published the results, which were both highly controversial and illuminating. Recently there have been cases of immigrant workers doing jobs that have led to their becoming contaminated with dangerous substances. It is very sad.

Health

Alcoholism According to social law (*Rechtsprechung*) alcoholism or drug or medicine addiction are regarded as illnesses (*Krankheiten*) and accordingly covered by the health insurance schemes. Insurance cover is lost however if an accident can be directly traced to the imbibing of alcohol. In this case, an accident at work is not considered as such but as something which is

Understanding Current Events

self-inflicted. This is what the book says, but it is well known that many manual workers, especially those who work in the open in all weathers, do drink a fair amount of beer and are thus scarcely sober. Where accidents occur and are recognised as such by the union, questions are seldom asked or insurance cover withheld. Presumably in cases of blatant drunkenness the worker would be warned and sacked before such an incident could occur. It would seem that in most alcohold-related accidents, insurance is rarely refused.

Drug addiction West Germany has, unfortunately, not been spared the tragedy of drug addiction; unscrupulous dealers hold sway over school children, junkies and the more sophisticated drug takers who manage to hold down a job while taking milder forms of drugs — for how long the milder forms is always the question. Ghastly photos of dead junkies lying in public lavatories after the last fatal fix are published in popular magazines. Respectable families are split when a son or daughter succumbs. Sadly, today this isn't new in western society and West Germany is certainly no exception. Private Eye films — *Derrick* and *The Kommissar* — bring the awful truth of drug addiction in realistically portrayed fictional form to the family television screen.

German police are meticulous and dedicated in their efforts to control the situation. Municipal advisory and rescue clinics do their best. Many people however argue that certain milder forms of drugs should be legalised to reduce the associated element of crime. Many Germans join the colony of junkies in Amsterdam where the Dutch authorities turn a blind eye to soft drugs, although such drug-taking is still against the law. To sum up, drug addiction remains an unresolved problem. It is estimated that in the Federal Republic a third of the money used by addicts to buy drugs is 'earned' through crime: mugging, burglary, prostitution and the like.

Energy
The problem with giving up nuclear power (*Kernenergie*) is that other sources of energy — coal, gas and oil — emit an unhappily high rate of carbon dioxide (*Kohlendioxyd*), a major contributor to the so-called glass house effect (*Treihauseffekt*)

Understanding Current Events

which is increasing the Earth's temperature and melting ice at the poles, and could thus ultimately raise the level of the sea by between 30 and 120cm (12 to 48in) etc. If the Federal Republic gives up nuclear energy, it will hardly be able to influence those countries that do use it to improve their safety standards. The problems of nuclear energy are international rather than national problems, like so many other worries in the European Community.

Demography
The birth rate has been falling and since 1974 has no longer kept pace with the death rate, although there are signs that the situation is changing – certainly immigrant workers have a rising birth rate.

16
German Culture

Different meanings of the word 'Kultur' and culture
There is nothing more daunting than German culture (*deutsche Kultur*). The word *Kultur* has a broader and deeper meaning than 'culture' in English. The ministries of education in the *Länder* were usually called *Kultursministerien*, ministries of culture. To English ears this may have George Orwellian undertones, but there is nothing sinister. Culture is recognised as a cause, an ideal, requiring vast subsidies, since in the television age the theatres would be left empty were patrons to be charged economic prices (though museums and art galleries charge admission except, in some cases, on Sundays). *Kultur* is not just connected with education but, as in English, connotes spiritual and other values which, unlike in English, mean something special to be taken very seriously indeed.

Old university towns have *Philosophenwege*, where presumably professors and students or scholarly citizens could discuss erudite subjects. It may be significant how many great German minds — poets and patrons of the arts, thinkers such as Nietzsche, Hölderlin, Ludwig II — crossed the boundary between genius and insanity.

The British don't mention the word 'culture' as often as Germans do. In fact the word means different things to English- and to German-speaking people. British imperialists did not assume responsibility of a fifth of the globe ostensibly to spread knowledge of Shakespeare, Milton and Marlowe (the word of God, perhaps), and certainly not British Culture with a large C. Germans did to some extent, albeit in a much smaller area in the South Seas and later, in the scramble for Africa. *Kultur* for them meant a way of life, not just as in English 'intellectual development'. *Kultur* includes behaviour and during the apogee of Nazism was treated as racial superiority. Now it has become less mystic, but still there is a hallowed ring to the term which is absent in English. It is very easy and a great temptation to

German Culture

generalise here, but personal experience suggests the following: Germans love abstract thought and attach a greater importance to theory than British people do. This is especially so in the humanities at university. It is also an expression of the well-ordered way they have of doing things, of going into great detail.

Kant, Hegel, Schopenhauer and Nietzsche provide an impressive philosophical heritage of scholarship, although one should not forget the astringent impulses given to British philosophers, especially Bertrand Russell, by the Austrian thinker Ludwig Wittgenstein and the Vienna Circle. Post-war existentialists, such as Martin Heidegger and Karl Jaspers, gave a new direction to German philosophy. They were also influenced by the *Frankfurter Schule* (Frankfurt School), principally by Max Horkheimer and Ernst Bloch who combined in their *kritische Theorie* Marxist social criticism with psychology. Other less politically but more generally motivated thinkers, such as the nuclear physicist Werner Heisenberg, propagated the use of science and resources in the cause of peace. Heisenberg's pupil, Carl Friedrich von Weizsäcker, argued in the same direction. German scholarship is exhaustingly rigorous and exact. Nothing is done by halves, but confusion is sometimes undeniably rife in some learned minds. The British scholar strives for clarity, the German for profundity.

The German passion for abstract thinking, whilst providing an excellent tool for intellectual analysis, can unnecessarily complicate relatively simple matters, or so it would seem. Possibly it is allied to the German penchant for making tortuous bureaucratic mountains out of everyday molehills (see The Post Office, pp114–17, and *Stempel*, p125). It may also find expression in the complexity of the language, particularly in the twists and turns of literary expression.

Goethe is revered, not only as a great poet but as a great thinker. In fact he wrote the first lines of *Faust* in so-called *Knittelvers* (doggerel). His mellifluous verse invests his dramas with great beauty. However, the so-called literary scientists (*Literaturewissenschaftler*) concentrate less on the aesthetics of Goethe's verse than on the ideas contained therein. It is Goethe the scholar and thinker rather than Goethe the poet to whom scholars devote their time. Nobody seems concerned with his

German Culture

very vigorous sex life, for example composing a poem whilst testing out the metre by drumming his fingers on a young lady's bare back in bed! Perhaps this may explain the recent student resistance to the works of Goethe and Schiller in favour of more modern writers, (though a dedicated teacher can motivate his pupils to accept the classics). Post-war German guilt-ridden preoccupation with the last war and Fascism has yielded to a concern with armaments and nuclear power stations. On the one hand there is 'Establishment-Kultur' — culture represented by the decorative and often most expensively restored theatres, richly filled museums and art galleries with the word spread on TV and radio programmes. On the other hand, there is a more diverse range of alternative anti-Establishment culture, essentially forms of protest against a variety of existing or imagined ills.

Literature

Before and during the last war several writers, notably Hermann Hesse, Thomas and Heinrich Mann, and Carl Zuckmayer, emigrated to America and wrote so-called emigration literature. Post-war preoccupation with past horrors produced a revolution in German literature, the *Gruppe 47* (Group 47), Berthold Brecht anti-theatre (*Verfremdungseffekt*), the rejection of theatrical illusion, and Wolfgang Borchert's drama of disillusionment '*Draußen vor der Tür*'. Heinrich Böll and Günter Grass wrote satiric novels full of social questioning, and bitter-sweet social and political analyses. Then there were Max Frisch's comic satires and Rolf Hochhuth's damning plays of Churchill and Pope Pacelli (Pius XII). Rainer-Werner Faßbinder, who died recently of an overdose of drugs, was in his films even more brittle and anarchistic despite his deeply sensitive personality. It is of course absurd to try and sum up half a century of German literature in a few words or slogans, but it is legitimate to suggest that it represents an agonizing over the past and a troubled questioning of the present. One hesitates to talk of the 'German soul' of Wagnerian dimensions, but modern German literature gives the impression of being essentially cerebral with an unsettling, querying and questioning social commentary. This is, however, not to deny the sheer artistry of Böll and Grass.

German Culture

Fringe culture
What bedevils expressions of alternative and fringe culture is the political past and not the uncertain nuclear future, whether the latter is concerned with energy for domestic uses or military purposes. Germany has become the potential cockpit of Europe and the authority of the State is no longer as strong as it was. Hence it is difficult to know what is purely Leftist, indeed Communist inspired and what is a sincere concern for the direction society is heading. Leftists shouldn't be denied sincere social concern, but how can their violence be justified, however sincere its perpetrators?

Historically, there was a rich tradition of Berlin cabaret critique against the Establishment and courageous satire aimed at the Nazis which, of course, received its expected retribution. Today the Berlin *'Lach- und Schieß-Gesellschaft'* (Mirth and Gibe Society) is a worthy follower of erstwhile satirists.

Satiric magazines like *Pardon* and *Titanic* also bite, though they are much less cruel than *Private Eye*.

German TV has no equivalent of *Spitting Image* or *Yes Minister* and public figures are not, as Germans would say, 'durch den Dreck gezogen' (dragged through the dirt) in the manner employed by *Private Eye*. The law offers greater protection to the individual than in Britain. The different parliamentary tradition in Britain usually causes politicians, especially ministers, to resign more-or-less immediately there is a hint of scandal. In Germany, unless it is absolutely clear where responsibility lies, they do not always do so. Franz-Josef Strauß was a case in point. He stood and fought his accusers (principally Rudolf Augstein, editor of the magazine *Der Spiegel*) who slung as much mud as they could at him, but nothing could be proved in court, so he survived and then (in Bavaria) went from strength to strength. However at a Federal level he was not so revered and was an unsuccessful candidate for the Chancellorship in the Federal election of 1982.

Mobile Theatre
An interesting experiment has recently been tried out whereby a small theatre company performs a play in someone's home. Thirty people are invited to watch the performance which takes place in the drawing room. Perhaps the idea will catch on.

German Culture

Art galleries and museums
Most State galleries are open on Sundays and entrance on that day is free. The earlier one arrives, the less crowded it will be. Catalogues are obtainable in English as are sometimes cassette guides which you can hire before going round. The same holds for local museums which open on a Sunday morning and at that time are often empty. Be careful to walk around the collection in the direction of the arrow (the *Führungslinie*). By noticing such things you assimilate a bit of local culture too!

Eßkultur: Cooking
You may of course try to maintain British cuisine in Germany: bacon (*Schinkenspeck*) and eggs, cereals and toast, marmalade with tea or coffee for breakfast, a hot meal for lunch and supper, but this is becoming pretty old-fashioned. But you might well be tempted at least to try the German way — breakfast (*Frühstück*) consisting of rolls and butter with cold meats, cheese and/or jam, and filtered coffee; lunch — a hot meal, often eaten at work in the canteen; and *Abendbrot* (supper) which traditionally is bread, rolls, cold meats and cheese, with tea with rum in it; or a hot meal. The main difference is breakfast or *Frühstück* which is usually taken earlier than in the UK because people begin work earlier (see p83). It is usually a very moderate meal compared with the traditional British breakfast. Lunch is usually at 12 noon and not at 1 o'clock as in the UK and the States. The evening meal could well just be *Abendbrot*. Sunday lunch is often the main meal of the week with roast pork or beef, but German meat tastes different from English because cattle receive different feed and the meat, following slaughter, is butchered differently.

Availability of British provisions
Certain kinds of British provisions are available in supermarkets and shops: English marmalade, ham, peanut butter and especially tea, but are usually appreciably dearer than at home. Cereals are available too, but Marmite is not, though on occasion one may find Oxo. There is no Hovis but many different kinds of white, brown and black bread are available. The same amount of variety holds for sausages.

   In general, few people pine for essentially English food, except

German Culture

possibly Marmite or digestive and ginger biscuits. Tea, which most English-speaking people tend to make with tea-bags, is available but its taste depends on the local water. Germans drink it much weaker than at home. After a time you tend to be converted to coffee which, apart from beer or wine (depending on the region), is the national drink and usually drunk filtered.

Shopping
Shopping in any country is at two levels: the major, costly, infrequent purchases (furniture, electrical goods, motor cars — already discussed) and everyday food and essentials. Germany is no exception and as elsewhere, time and money can be saved by shopping in supermarkets. Milk, bread and meat are not usually delivered (unlike the UK), and there is little opportunity to buy food outside closing hours. Moreover with so many public holidays you may rush out for bread in the morning and find the shop closed! As already mentioned there is considerable trade union opposition to the relaxing of closing hours. In the large cities there are usually shops at the main railway stations that sell groceries and bread; officially they are meant just for travellers, but locals find them useful too, even if the price range is higher than in the ordinary shops. There is the added advantage that goods sold at the station are usually fresh, which is very useful over long weekends where several public holidays have been tacked onto the usual free time.

Major, one-time purchases require considerable thought and much shopping around if you are to save money. And you *can* save quite a lot.

Food and shopping: eating and drinking
The clichéd picture of beer-swilling Germans eating sausages is misleading. In any case, eating out in Germany has recently become more cosmopolitan and sophisticated, and this also applies in most English-speaking countries.

You will in time find your own favourite restaurants and in your cooking will make the best of what is available in the shops. This is not the place for a detailed description of German cuisine, which more useful to a tourist. For most Germans, except those on expense accounts, eating out in expensive restaurants is a treat or confined to holidays.

The emphasis here is on normal German eating and drinking habits. First a few general remarks and hints. German food is not for weight-watchers. It tends to be fattening. Much of it is fried or grilled. Vegetables are well seasoned and often mixed with butter (drenched is a better word). Spinach is served as a seasoned, buttered purée. Bread, potato and sausage appear in many varieties — there are hundreds of different types of bread varying in colour, taste and substance, sweet and salty; in loaves or rolls, latterly containing roughage (*Ballast*), but not a great deal of taste. Potatoes, introduced into Germany in the eighteenth century, are eaten boiled (*Salzkartoffeln*), fried or sautéed, or they are shredded to make dumplings or mixed with milk to make potato purée — *Kartoffelpuffer, mit Apfelmus* (with apple purée) – or potato salad.

Sausages constitute a cuisine of their own, with hundreds of different kinds throughout the country with many regional variations, from the Munich *Weißwurst* (white sausage) to the *Frankfurter*. Salami type sausages are sold by the slice and when shopping the worst thing that can happen when in a hurry is to get behind a *Hausfrau* (housewife) in the queue who is buying small amounts of different kinds of sausage. It takes ages with each amount being weighed to the nearest gram. One reassuring thing: food shops are usually spotlessly clean and there is no smell of dead meat as in some English butchers' shops. Sausage can be eaten warm or as cold meat. The latter, together with cold cooked ham, often forms the base of *Abendbrot* (high tea).

Butchers no longer slaughter their own meat. Slaughtering is done centrally under the supervision of a vet who also examines the meat for quality and hormones etc. Meat not passed for human consumption is sold at the so-called *Freibank* as pet food.

Dogs are not allowed in shops. There are special rings outside to which dog owners can attach the lead.

Bread, potato and sausage can form a staple diet for some Germans, especially at lunch time when many an office or manual worker takes out his sausage sandwich, ie, sausage in a roll — *Wurstbrot* — which is not the same as a sausage roll. Earlier still for the early morning break (*Brotzeit*) workers fortify themselves with *Wurstbrote* and beer — more about beer later.

This is the background against which many Germans buy food. They are not great ones for fresh salads (often drenched in dressing) or puddings (*Nachtische*), regarding the former as consisting of a few leaves of salad an beetroot, bottled celery and red cabbage, and the latter as *Apfelstrudel* (which can be delicious warm), *Früchtebecher* (ice cream with lumps of tinned fruit covered with whipped cream), *Apfelringe* (frittered slices of apple) or *Weincreme* (a soufflé-like mixture). There are no warm fruit pies and very few warm puddings of any sort.

This doesn't mean to say you can't buy salad or fruit and alter the menu to satisfy individual taste at home. Italian vegetables with Italian, Greek, Spanish and Israeli fruit are readily available at affordable prices. In adjusting English eating habits to German, it is more enterprising to experiment with local cuisine and supplement it with salad and fruit, perhaps cutting down on starchy foods, such as bread and potatoes, as well as the fatty types of meat and sausage.

German meat does taste different in some instances. There is no roast beef as such, that is with Yorkshire pudding and roast potatoes. There is *Rostbeef* (roast beef), which is usually served as a cold meat. Meat is also cooked differently. When it is roasted in the oven, some fat is used, but by occasionally pouring a little water over the meat, it is tenderised in the cooking. A gravy-like sauce (*Sauce*) is then made out of the residual fat to which is added broth made from soup bones (*Suppenknochen*), seasoning and spices.

Instead of roast potatoes, dumplings (*Knödel or Klöße*), of which there are several different kinds ranging from the potato to the bread type, are served. *Böhmischer Knödel* (Bohemian dumpling) is of light texture; there is also a Bavarian variety which is delightful to eat with sauce poured on top and down the middle which has been gently prised open. It is deliciously filling and you can easily be seduced into overeating and consequently feel embarrassed when the *Knödel* begin to swell inside your stomach making you feel distinctly less mobile than before. Beware! I had a greedy friend who almost exploded after eating four; stick to two and you will survive!

To balance the *Knödel* it is a joy to sample the different types of cabbage (*Kraut*) in addition to the traditional English light green kind which is usually served raw and pickled. White cabbage may be either cooked and pickled or served raw, mixed with spices and herbs. The red cabbage cooked and served warm is delicious; it is either cut into strands or served as a semi-purée mixed with apple making it taste sweet.

German soups are delicious but tend to be fattening. In the north the most typical is *Ochsenschwanzsuppe* (oxtail) and in the south *Gulaschsuppe* (goulash soup). *Kartoffelsuppe* (potato soup), *Pfannkuchensuppe* (omelette soup) and *Brühe* (broth with egg yolk) are also very tasty.

Pastries and cakes German cakes are seductive and tasty, and you'll enjoy regional specialities such as Bavarian *Zwetschendatschi* (Damson cake) and *Schwäbischer Apfelkuchen* (Swabian apple cake), *Schwarzwälderkirschtorte* (Black Forest gâteau) and for Christmas *Plätzchen* (biscuits and shortbread). Good standbys are *Apfelkuchen* (apple cake), *Käsekuchen* (cheese cake), *Obstkuchen* (fruit flan) and *Rot- oder Schwarzbeerkuchen* (red- or blackcurrant cake). Try them out but remember your waistline.

German pastry differs from English; the flour (*Mehl*) is milled in a different way, it rises less reliably in the oven, and the processing uses more ingredients.

Milk German milk is pasteurised as in England, and milk is also homogenised. German milk is not as creamy as most British. More of the fat has been extracted to produce other milk products such as *Joghurt* or *Quark*, a kind of cottage cheese. A special type of condensed milk, which functions more as cream rather than milk, is used in both coffee and tea (many people drink their tea 'black' or 'clear' with a slice of lemon).

Water Tap water is neither served nor drunk in restaurants or at home. Local water, which varies from district to district, usually contains chlorine or additives which render it tasteless. Mineral waters are very popular and their consumption is increasing all the time.

As already explained, the quality of the water unfortunately affects the taste of tea and it is as well to buy either specially blended tea at a specialist tea and coffee shop or to mix *Earl Grey* with any quality of tea. At least you will be able to taste it. Germans usually serve tea very weak.

Non-alcoholic drinks are available in profusion ranging from

German Culture

the American Cokes to the local apple juice (*Apfelsaft*), grape juice (*Traubensaft*) and other conventional fruit juices.

Beer Beer is a national drink in most parts of the Federal Republic and in Bavaria is regarded as ordinary nourishment. German beer is brewed according to recipes dating from the Middle Ages, especially regarding the purity of the malt and hops. Until recent Common Market legislation, foreign beer brewed under less stringent regulations was not allowed to be sold in the country. Now following a ruling in the European Court, foreign beer may not be excluded from West Germany and is available as well. The same holds for foreign sausage.

Wine Wine is drunk throughout the country but grown in the Rhineland and in Franconia. German wine tends to be sweeter than French, and less red wine is made. However, German wine has its devotees and is certainly well worth drinking. There are special wine tours of the vineyards and quite respectable wines can be bought in supermarkets.

Wine is not just a drink; a certain social drinking significance is also attached to it. It is customary in the north to seal the signing of a contract with a glass of wine.

Coffee German coffee is usually filtered and each cup (*Tasse*) or pot (*Kännchen*) is prepared separately. It is not left to stew as sometimes in English-speaking countries. However it is not cheap; a cup in a normal café or even in a pub costs on average DM 2,-. Excellent cups of coffee can be obtained much more cheaply at *Kaffeeausschänken* (coffee shops), which are run by the main coffee roasters to sell their own brands. Here you stand at little round tables to drink coffee and buy biscuits; sometimes you can pick up special bargain offers, from clocks and watches to bathrobes and books. The *Kaffeeausschank* is a typically German institution and well worth a visit.

17
Relaxation

The Wirtshaus and Lokal

Eating and drinking out is very much a social and corporate occasion, more so than in English-speaking countries. True, there are no pubs in the English sense where people can stand or sit at the bar. Usually there is no bar as such but a counter, where drinks are dispensed to staff who then serve customers seated at tables. Regulars have their own table, known as the *Stammtisch*. This type of German pub, called a *Wirtshaus*, is patronised by the locals. Hot meals and snacks are also served, so that it has the dual function of an unpretentious restaurant (though the food may be excellent) as well as a pub for drinking; it often remains open until midnight and after.

Higher up the price scale is the *Lokal* which usually has a bar, a *Diskothek* (disco), even a *Kapelle* (band). One talks of a *Bier* (beer) *lokal* or a *Wein* (wine) *lokal*. Meals may also be served at tables. Some *Lokale* (beer cellars) are fairly large and are not necessarily underground. Some very famous ones, mostly in Munich, are in general owned by the major breweries.

Eating and drinking out

The nice thing about eating or drinking out is the ritual of courtesy that this involves. You say 'Guten Abend' ('Good evening') upon entering a *Wirtshaus* or *Lokal* and some guests will reply 'Guten Abend'. A gentleman always enters before the lady to see if everything is all right. Only in a very exclusive restaurant will you have to wait for the maître d'hôtel to show you to your place. If it is very full and places are only available at tables already occupied by other guests, then it is polite to ask: 'Ist dieser Platz frei?' ('Is this place free?') before sitting down.

After serving you the waiter or waitress will usually say, 'Guten Appetit' ('I hope you like it'), friends wish one another

Relaxation

'Einen guten Hunger' ('I hope it makes you hungry'). You answer, 'Thank you'.

When your plate is collected for the next course, you will hear, 'Hat es Ihnen geschmeckt? ('Did you like it?') – or 'Hoffentlich hat es Ihnen geschmeckt' ('I hope you liked it'). And you answer, even if it tasted dreadful (that is, if you don't want to complain), 'Ja, danke.' ('Yes, thank you.') The more exclusive the restaurant, the less likely the waiter or waitress will be to indulge in such pleasantries, because it will be assumed that you are going to or will have enjoyed your meal.

Cafés — sometimes restaurants too — are wonderful places to sit and read the magazines and newspapers usually provided; nobody minds if you just sit and read over a cup of coffee. You are never given the feeling of having outstayed your welcome unless there is a shortage of tables.

Tipping

Tipping is an art in most countries and Germany is no exception. Generally tipping is appreciated and expected and is based on the credo, even among the professional classes, that no-one does anything for nothing unless the recipient of a service or favour is a relation or a close friend. The tradition of unpaid service to the community hardly exists. People are in general more commercially minded. I have given someone a lift and had DM 5 thrust into my hand, which I found most embarrassing.

In restaurants and cafés the *Bedienungsgeld* (service) is included in the bill as in the tax (*Mehrwertsteuer*), but it is the custom in a café to round up a modest bill for DM 2,20 to DM 2,50 or from 3,80 to DM 4 — thus to the nearest 50 Pfennig or 1 DM. In a more expensive restaurant where the bill might come to DM 94, you would round it up to DM 100. Taxi drivers expect the same. Railway or airport porters do not exist. Trolleys are available at airports and railway stations; sometimes they cost DM 1 to hire. Caretakers and newspaper roundsmen (or women) also expect a tip at Christmas but do not always get it. Petrol pump attendants who do not always expect a few Pfennigs sometimes receive them. In hotels gratuities really are included in the service charge added to the bill, though if you are particularly satisfied with the chambermaid — often a foreign *Gastarbeiter* (see p160) — a tip will be appreciated.

Relaxation

Commissionaires only exist at the most exclusive hotels and they expect and receive gratuities.

It may seem hard to say this, but Germans do not appreciate receiving something for nothing. If you do a colleague a favour, usually he or she will want to reciprocate with a box of chocolates or a bottle of wine. Whilst it is polite to say 'Oh you shouldn't have bothered' on no account refuse the offering but say how much you enjoyed helping out. I say 'usually' because there are others who are somewhat unscrupulous in exploiting foreign colleagues, especially at universities (see *Doing favours*, p137).

Entertaining

Germans do entertain at home but usually only personal friends and acquaintances, rather than business or academic colleagues. Business people tend to take guests to restaurants, rather than invite them home. Germans are not inhospitable, but home is more for the family and there is, as already mentioned, a division between family and business. To be invited to a German home for a meal is therefore a special mark of respect and a genuine expression of friendship. You must also remember that usually both husband and wife work and that the effort required to prepare the meal is correspondingly greater than when the wife is at home all day.

It is customary for guests to take a bunch of flowers, being sure to unwrap them before handing them over, which requires great manual dexterity. Be punctual; there is no English 7.30 for 8. For whatever time you are invited, arrive promptly because that is probably when the meal is to be served. The other important difference in Germany is usually that the more you enjoy yourself, the longer you are expected to stay, assuming of course that your host and hostess are not yawning their heads off. The idea of leaving at 10.30, at the latest 11 pm, is foreign to Germans; when reciprocating with German friends don't be surprised if they stay half the night. It is a very natural approach. People are not formal any more.

Where you can get caught out is with an invitation to a wine or beer party. You might imagine that a buffet supper would be served, but you are offered mainly nuts, cheese straws and open sandwiches. This doesn't always occur, but it can happen.

Relaxation

Drinking on an empty stomach at 8 in the evening and continuing for several hours can be dangerous, so it's advisable to inquire as tactfully as possible whether the invitation is just for drinks or if there is also a meal.

The corollary of this, which can be embarrassing if you are unprepared, is that if you invite Germans to an English-style sherry party from 6–8pm and people enjoy it, you may have guests until well past midnight and have to send out for food. Many Germans are unfamiliar with the idea of a pre-dinner sherry party, where those attending the sherry party are not expected to remain for dinner, so plan this sort of entertaining very carefully indeed, if you do not want to be put in an awkward position.

Commercial entertainment: TV and radio

Because of the language, commercial entertainment for most long stayers may at first consist of watching TV without understanding much. TV is, however, a good way of helping to learn the language and about the country too. In time it may pall. At present television is mainly in the hands of different *Anstalten des öffentlichen Rechts*; these are public corporations, by rights independent of the government of the *Länder* but when it comes to the appointment of leading figures (directors) and the raising of viewers' licence fees, in fact answerable to government. The *ZDF (Zweites Deutsches Fernsehen)* is a public corporation which transmits programmes to the regions. Some of these programmes are produced by the regions on a co-operative basis, for example the *ARD (Arbeitsgemeinschaft der öffentlich-rechtlichen Rundfunkanstalten der Bundesrepublik Deutschland)* programme. Private television is still in its infancy.

Generally the standard of West German television is uneven. This is partly because a shortage of funds has brought a subsequent reliance on quiz shows and American soap operas. As with much of the German film industry, a wealth of creativity may well exist but it rarely seems to find its way onto the screen.

This need not necessarily affect you because cable TV is gradually being introduced so that foreign programmes are available and even if they are not of the best quality, at least they are in English.

Eventually as your understanding of the language improves

you may well find that documentary programmes are the most interesting. All the *Länder* corporations have educational programmes and some are worthwhile. The same holds for radio programmes for schools. Radio, which requires a greater command of the language, in time could become a further source of entertainment. Finally, a combined TV and radio licence is obligatory and this can be paid for at any bank or post office.

Videos
If you plan to invest in a television set, the cheapest are very cheap, and it is better to buy a slightly larger and more expensive one with a video recorder so that you can hire films from the local video dealer who will usually have some cassettes in English. If the dealer scents a new market he may extend his selection of English-language films. As British cassettes fit German recorders, friends at home can also send over films. For American cassettes a special type of German TV set is required.

Entertainment: cinema
What holds for TV also holds for local cinema, but if the choice of cinema is limited in your town it is worth enquiring whether there is a cinema society (possibly at the local university) with a weekly showing of quality films. Sometimes the local church, school or nearest British Council has a film club worth joining. This will give you the opportunity to meet people too.

Coffee and cakes
The first stage of being invited to someone's home is often the invitation to Sunday afternoon coffee and cakes, sometimes starting with a walk in the country. Take some flowers for your hostess (or chocolates or, if English, a packet of tea would be most appreciated). After the walk (if there is one) coffee and cakes will be served on the best china, with a neatly ironed table cloth with frilly borders. After consuming vast quantities of coffee and cakes, out will come the wine bottle, nuts and cheese straws and, before you know it, you are into an unheralded, second, more light-hearted form of gathering. If this goes well, you could well be invited to stay to *Abendbrot*. Finally, as you sway home brimful of good cheer and lashings of food, remember that you were only invited for coffee and cake! If you want to

avoid staying for too long but don't want to offend your hosts by getting up and leaving at 5.30, it is better to warn them *beforehand* and explain that unfortunately you have an appointment at 5.45 pm, then you can leave early without offending anyone. Of course if you want to stay on, then just wait and see what happens — once the bottles are uncorked and you are invited to stay on, you are really meant to.

Food and being overweight

Chronic food shortages during and following the war led people to overeat when food became readily available. The very high fat content in German cuisine (as mentioned above, much is either grilled or fried) has worsened the problem of an overweight population. The popularity of beer is an added problem — witness the number of so-called beer stomachs which you see about. Enthusiasm for sport — the *Trimm-Dich-fit* (keep fit movement), jogging, etc (though this leads to heart-attacks among some people), does help to counteract the problem of overweight. Unfortunately, it's a mere drop in the ocean. Inadequate public transport in rural districts has brought about dependence upon cars, which in turn discourages people from taking sufficient exercise.

Sport

Sport is taken seriously in Germany, judging by the number of sports clubs and the amount of sport shown on TV. The most popular sports are soccer and tennis, the latter being given a great boost by the success of local stars such as Boris Becker and Steffi Graf.

Germany must, in any case, be considered an eldorado for sportsmen, be they water enthusiasts sailing off the north coast and on the lakes, or skiers, hikers and walkers who have the most idyllic, picture postcard country to explore, in the *Schwarzwald* (Black Forest) and *Bayerischer Wald* (Bavarian Forest) as well as the *Fränkische Schweiz* (Franconian Switzerland) and numerous other places. Unlike England, or rather Scotland, one generally expects reasonable weather conditions (bright sunshine) while skiing in the mountains. It makes all the difference. Golf players will be pleased to know that golf courses are springing up everywhere in Germany and the clubs often employ British coaches. Squash has also become popular though it is an expensive sport as it was found not to be as commercially profitable as imagined. Some baseball is played and even cricket is starting up with teams in Berlin, Frankfurt and Munich.

There is no shortage of sports facilities in West Germany. Determined efforts are made to provide soccer pitches (*Bolzplätzen*) in residential areas to keep children off the streets. Many local sports clubs provide more special facilities: tennis, badminton, gymnastics and so on. Membership fees are usually within the reach of most people save where such clubs are of a more pronounced social nature and demand higher subscriptions. Long stayers should be able to find a sports club to fit their needs and pockets.

There are some 60,000 sports clubs with approximately 19 million members in the Federal Republic organised in *Länder* sports federations under 'the umbrella organisation' of the German Sports Federation (*Deutscher Sportbund, DSB*). It is reported that 'every third inhabitant of the Federal Republic is a member of a sports club'. However, sports clubs complete with statutes and committees tend to lose out to private fitness studios, which offer more modern facilities in a less regimented and more informal ambience.

Gardening

One way of feeling at home anywhere is to have your own garden. Many Germans have green fingers and are able to coax a veritable botanical garden out of the minutest plot, create magnificent window boxes and conjure up floral wonders in allotment gardens. You will miss English-quality grass lawns because the soil is not so damp as in UK. Lawns require considerable care and the results are often meagre, but more sun creates excellent flower gardens.

Pets

The good news for dog-owners is that, assuming your pet has all the necessary innoculation certificates (*Impfpass*), there is no problem about bringing it into the country. The only thing to watch, when living in the south, is the danger of your dog catching rabies. There are various explanations as to why this

Relaxation

dreaded disease has not been stamped out: it is spread by bats, by foxes and other wild animals; it is brought over from the Eastern bloc border countries, and so on. The important point is that it still exists and there is no cure, only prevention by innoculation.

You should be aware, when living in the country, that your dog may be stolen by *Hundefänger*, who apparently do their dirty business at dusk. They attract the poor animal with food and then catch it with the aid of a long stick or pole and noose. There is a vigorous campaign against using animals for experiments. Laboratories are broken into and animals used for testing are released. However, sadly, there doesn't appear to be any effective deterrent to the theft of pets. Dogs and cats should not be allowed to roam. You must look after them properly. Moreover, depending upon which part of the country you move to, there are certain diseases which are transmitted via domestic pets from foxes and mice to human beings. If a disease such as rabies goes undetected in the early stages, it can be terminal. It is not being alarmist to take great care of your pets.

Beware of dogs

Be careful! Beware of dogs, they bite! I have even been bitten in a café. People do not always have their dogs under proper control. They jump up at passers-by and bark ferociously. This can be quite frightening and irritating when the owner doesn't have the courtesy to apologise. Germans sometimes adore and spoil their dogs, at other times they treat them harshly, which may explain why a spoilt or badly treated dog may attack a stranger. If you have a dog it is as well to have third party insurance in case anything untoward happens.

Cats are different by nature and temperament. They are inoffensive creatures but are often spoilt. Some people offer a 'cat-sitting' service. They advertise in the local press. One such lady put my telephone number instead of hers in the newspaper and as a result I was inundated with calls from cat owners going on holiday!

Touring

Germany is a historical contradiction in terms: pre-1871, a loose confederation of independent kingdoms, principalities

Relaxation

and duchies; post-Bismarck's Empire until 1918, Prussian hegemony; thereafter the weak Weimar Republic; followed by Hitler's Reich which left two Germanies, one each side of an iron curtain, with the West German capital in Bonn while Berlin, an Allied-Russian responsibility, lies split between East and West. The contradictions multiply and are further multiplied by the regional diversity of Germany, especially the Federal Republic.

There is no such thing as touring Germany. You visit different sub-divided Germanies. Hamburg, in the north, is historically orientated towards England. It is claimed that the city is half-English. It is almost the only German city to have a traditional gentlemen's club such as those that abound in the States or the United Kingdom. Hamburg is best appreciated from the water on short pleasure trips; the beautiful Alster lake heightens the effect. On land, the impressive collection of museums and art galleries are inviting to the visitor; but he would do well to avoid the notorious red-light district, the *Reeperbahn*.

Most visitors to Germany go south — Cologne with its magnificent cathedral which took more than 400 years to complete; Heidelberg with its associations with *The Student Prince*, the German Romantic, Somerset Maugham and other writers. It is the Romantic which accompanies one down the Rhine with its castles and moments of poetic vision and remembrance. Germany is not just a country to visit. It has to be experienced too.

Even the commercial capital of Germany, Frankfurt, is a tourist Mecca, boasting a Goethe house, museums and art galleries. It was also the place where the emperors of the German Holy Roman Empire were crowned. The surrounding countryside is well worth visiting too, especially the Taunus.

Impressive as the sights are to the north and middle of Germany, it is usually the south, mainly Bavaria, to which most people gravitate, be they Germans or tourists. Every German student would like to study at Munich's Ludwig-Maximilian University. Most Germans have been skiing in the Bavarian Alps south of Munich and, of course, there can scarcely be a tourist to Germany who has not seen the dreamer King Ludwig's fairytale castles, inspired by veneration of Richard Wagner and his music. Munich, the capital city of Bavaria,

Relaxation

is definitely another tourist Mecca with its churches, palaces, galleries, museum and Bohemian quarter, the Schwabing. Ludwig's father, Ludwig I, redesigned the city and turned Munich into a mini-Athens. It was one of his sons, the hapless Otto, who for a short time became King of Greece before having to flee into exile. Ludwig built large boulevards and was thought to be mad. Today, with increased congestion, you appreciate how sane he was.

18
Staying On?

Introduction
Having settled down so well with a job, house and friends you begin to wonder whether staying on might not be the most sensible thing. Again, this is not an easy decision to take, though it might just resolve itself.

As with deciding to move to Germany, you might consider following the advice given in the first chapter (*Preparations*) in reverse. Take a good look at what you have achieved in Germany and decide whether you want to, or indeed can, give it up to return to life back home.

Life in Germany: futuristic guesswork — Aufenthaltsgenehmigung versus Aufenthaltsberechtigung
Those wishing to stay in Germany for more than three months require an *Aufenthaltsgenehmigung* (residence permit) which, for some Europeans, is now allied to the Common Market identity card. The procedure is not too complicated. You are required to produce the following documents at the *Einwohnermeldeamt* (Citizens Register Office):
1. Valid passport (make sure it's not about to run out)
2. Photo
3. Work contract
4. Certificate (*Führungszeugnis*) from the *Bundeszentralregister* in Berlin confirming that you have no previous convictions
5. Clean bill of health

Usually the first *Aufenthaltsgenehmigung* will be granted for a year when it has to be renewed. After a longer stay the *Einwohnermeldeamt* will usually extend it for a number of years – perhaps after you have been in the country for a few years, and then for an unlimited period.

After a longer stay, it might be worthwhile considering applying for an *Aufenthaltsberechtigung* which is more than

183

Staying On?

permission to stay, it is the *right* to stay. It may be granted after eight years in the Federal Republic and for this the following documents are required:
1. Valid passport (again, please ensure it is not about to run out)
2. Copy of your *Mietvertrag* (rent contract)
3. Certificate from the local court (*Amtsgericht*) that you are not in debt
4. Work permit
5. Salary certificate (*Verdienstbescheinigung*) for two years
6. Certificate showing that children under 14 are being looked after (*Kinderaufsicht*)
7. Certificate that children attend school (*Schulbescheinigung*)
8. Pension certificate (*Rentenversicherungsnachweis*)
9. Health certificate (*Gesundheitserklärung*)

Applying for German citizenship

After ten years (less in special cases) you can apply for German citizenship – which means surrendering your own. You will obviously want to think *very* carefully before doing this. It might make you feel more at home in Germany and give you greater job protection. However, on your death your estate will become liable to German tax, which might be less onerous than British, though for the sake of convenience this may depend upon whether or not your dependants have assumed German citizenship too — see *Making your will*, p25.

Broader horizons

Moving to Germany, however specialist an undertaking this may be, can also open windows on a more international way of life. You can use Germany as a starting point for visiting and exploring other parts of Europe. There is no longer the Atlantic or the Channel between home and the continent. You are already on it, and moving to Germany and making a life home there can thus transform your own way and perspective of life.

It is in this mood that this book is written, as a means of introducing Germany and how to get settled in but also how to use your time there to readjust to a different way of life that offers wider horizons than hitherto. Don't allow life in Germany to become so intense that you miss out on the European delights that are literally on your doorstep.

Staying On?

Low crime rate
One pleasant thing about living in Germany is the relatively low rate of crime compared to the States or to some parts of the United Kingdom. Of course, there are problems with drug related offences in the large cities where in certain districts, like *Kreuzberg* in West Berlin or *Hafenstraße* in Hamburg, anti-social elements seem to rule the roost. In general the crime rate is much lower and while thefts take place in small towns, they are mercifully few.

The general awareness of crime makes one sympathetic to the German obsession with keys and locking everything up.

Old age pension
The following holds if you have joined the German pension system. For many, the old age pension is payable at the earliest from 60 and later from 65 years of age (though there is talk of increasing the retiring age to 67) onwards. It depends on your state of health and for how long you have contributed. If you are 60 and are an invalid or otherwise unable to work *and* have 35 '*anrechnungsfähige Versicherungsjahre*' (years which count for the pension), 15 of which have been *Versicherungszeit* (the period you were insured), the pension is payable. If you are 63 and have fulfilled the conditions mentioned above, the pension is payable too. When taking a pension earlier than 65 there are restrictions as to how much you may earn without deduction from the pension. You may not earn for more than two months in a year and then on an average no more than DM 1,000 a month. Invalids are restricted until the age of 62, except that they may only earn DM 500 a month on average.

On reaching 65 and thereafter, pension is payable assuming that you have been insured for a minimum of five years. There are no restrictions on supplementary earnings.

For a woman a pension is payable from the age of 60, on condition that she has been insured for 15 years and that for the previous 20 years at least 121 months' contributions (*Pflichtbeiträge*) have been paid. She may continue working under certain conditions. Such earnings may not exceed an average of DM 440 monthly or be for a period of more than two months ie, 50 working days per annum, until she is 65

Staying On?

when she can work as much as she wants without suffering a drop in pension.

Those who are unemployed and 60 years old and have been insured for 15 years and can show that they have been unemployed for at least 52 weeks during the last 18 months, and have been (*Pflichtbeitragszeiten*[1]) for 8 of the last 10 years, receive a pension. This period of 10 years is extended when there have been periods of unemployment and illness (*Ausfallzeiten*). The pensioner is permitted to work for up to two months ie, 50 days and earn a monthly average of DM 440. If he or she resumes employment, the pension is discontinued but, if unemployed again, it is resumed.

Health insurance

After contributions to obligatory health insurance for some time, Germans have to decide whether to have *Privat* or *Gesetzliche Krankenversicherung* (private or obligatory health insurance). A long stayer who has contributed to the *Gesetzliche Krankenversicherung* has to list former illnesses if he applies to join a private health scheme. If you miss out a particular illness which can be connected with a later medical problem whilst you are insured, the insurance company will refuse to pay anything. If you — as you should — list all former illnesses you may have to pay extra premiums to cover the risk of renewed illness. You should be especially on your guard against private insurers and reps who suggest that it is not necessary to mention every single illness you have had. As following this advice reduces the premiums payable some people believe the insurance agent. However, 'mundliche Absprachen' (verbal agreements) are not legally binding. Only what is down in black and white in the contract counts. Even if the agent adds his particular concession in writing it has no effect because the contract is so worded that nothing in the contract may be contrary to the general conditions of business (*allgemeine Geschäftsbedingungen*) laid down by the company.

With *Ersatzkrankenkassen* the father's insurance covers the

---

1 *Beitragszeiten*: periods for which monthly contributions are paid either *pflicht* or *freiwillig*

children. With private insurance, children must be insured separately.

Private insurance schemes, though cheaper than the *Krankenkassen* or *Ersatzkassen*, do not reduce premiums for old age pensioners, which is when the health insurance may be most needed. As *gesetzliche Krankenkasse* premiums are fixed according to income, the premium should be less on retirement. Finally, once you leave the *gesetzliche Krankenversicherung* you may not rejoin it unless your income falls below the *Beitragsbemessungsgrenze* when insurance is no longer voluntary but obligatory.

Health

The average life span of women in the Federal Republic was in 1988 78.5 and for males 71.9. Smoking (active and passive), alcohol and the high consumption of fat are major health risk factors. Whilst 47.3 per cent of smokers are male as compared to 31.1 per cent female, the percentage of younger female smokers in the 30 to 39 age group is 43.8 per cent. Middle aged and older men tend progressively to give up smoking: of the 50 to 59 age group only 42.3 per cent smoke, and of the 60 to 69 only 37.8 per cent that is of those who are still alive!

Pensions

The older you get, the more interesting the subject of pensions becomes. State pensions usually pay pensioners 60 to 70 per cent of their previous salary or wage. This places great strains upon the State especially in the future when the percentage of pensioners compared to the working population will be extremely high.

Wage-earners receive their pensions from the *LVA* (*Landesversicherungsanstalt*), salary earners (*Angestellte*) from the *BfA* (*Bundesversicherungsanstalt für Angestellte*) from Berlin, and officials (*Beamte*) from the Federal, *Länder* or local governments.

In West Germany pensions are mainly paid by the State. The government has only recently been urging people to insure themselves privately as well. In general, people rely upon the State pension. The system is not simple but has its own logic which is fair enough: work long enough and pay in enough and

Staying On?

you will obtain the full pension (although certain extenuating circumstances are recognised). Basically you must have been in the system for a while, the waiting period (*Anwärterzeit*), and you must be 65 years old (the general retirement age). Once the qualifying period has elapsed, you may claim a pension.

Obviously there is a distinction between the old age pension, which assumes the *Anwärterzeit*, and invalid pensions due to illness, accident or other causes which render work impossible, and unemployment benefit.

Old age

Considerable effort is made by the authorities at *Länder* and municipal level to ensure that the old are not forgotten. As in all industrial societies, senior citizens who live alone because of the death of a spouse (and where children or grandchildren live far away) present a problem. Time tends to weigh heavily on such old people's hands. Although facilities are provided — a meeting place where they may drink coffee and talk — and possibly also have the services of a counsellor if required, many old people do not bother to attend.

The cold is a problem too, but many authorities provide *Wärmestuben* where senior citizens can spend the day out of the cold.

Accommodation allowance (Wohngeld)

Should you fall on hard times, the State provides assistance with rent and accommodation costs for needy cases. The State emphasises that this is not a form of charity but the right of every citizen. It depends upon the size of the family, of income and of rent. A compensatory benefit allowance (*Lastenzuschuß*) can be paid to the owner-occupier, as opposed to a tenant. German allowances (*Familienfreibeiträge*) are subtracted from the family income, and other sources of income, such as children's allowance (*Kindergeld*), are also not regarded as income. Various groups of people, such as invalids (*Aussiedler* and *Heimkehrer*), also have certain amounts exempted. The rent (*Miete*) also includes the ancillary costs (*Nebenkosten*).

Passing on

Death cannot be avoided, but life in retirement can be more enjoyable if you have settled your affairs and made certain preparations. Some people enjoy living in a foreign country but do not want to die there or express the desire, if they do, to be buried at home. Such matters should be taken into consideration. As German health regulations are very strict in this respect and local burial (as opposed to cremation) is very expensive, it is as well to make the necessary financial and administrative preparations well in advance. Unless you have given clear instructions to the contrary in your will — and this is obtainable locally (or instructions may have been left with your local bank or the British Consulate) — after a comparatively short time you will be under German earth.

First it is essential, particularly for Americans who are used to another funeral culture, to understand the German attitude to death in relation to the remains. Cremation is becoming more widespread: more than half of those who die are cremated in some areas. The remainder are buried in municipal or interdenominational church cemeteries.

Moreover, your family cannot own a plot in perpetuity, apart from those whose family plots were bought before the war, but usually only rent it for twenty years, after which the contract regulating everything has to be renewed. You can arrange to have the grave looked after by a local gardener who will even put flowers on it on special occasions. Apparently the system works very well.

What can one do?
Retirement is not easy for some people and possibly more difficult abroad where you could easily have the feeling of not being wanted or needed enough. Nowadays people feel and look younger and fitter than they used to and do not want to feel left on the shelf. Retirement is the time to do those things you never had time to do before.

For some, further education (*Volkshochschule*) springs to mind; there in the evenings you can learn a language or a variety of subjects. This might be an opportunity to brush up on your German and meet others in the same situation.

Others might consider writing. Writing is, of course, a grossly overcrowded profession, but there is always room for those with something new to say. Living abroad produces useful material for writing, for example (I hope) this book!

Staying On?

Returning home: the procedure in reverse
Returning home may not always be entirely voluntary. You could stay on longer, but are worried that by staying too long re-adjustment may become too difficult or well-nigh impossible. Obviously, if you have enjoyed living in Germany, it will be a wrench to leave. However there could be a best-of-both worlds possible, which will be considered later on.

At present you are concerned with winding up everything to effect a smooth return home without too many loose ends.

First, continuation of employment, if you have been merely on secondment, is no problem; but if you have worked for a different company in Germany or have tried a different line altogether, you may find things difficult. Depending upon your profession or position, it may be hard to find the German equivalent at home. So much so that you may not want to leave Germany and return home on spec to look for a job. All this is obvious, but less obvious is the exiled effect which everyone who has lived abroad for a long period experiences. You think you still know your own country through and through but you don't any longer. You may see it as an extension of your life abroad, you remember things as they were, and everything has moved on since then. It could be that having benefitted from a higher standard of living in Germany, you may not find it psychologically easy to settle down again at home, whether as a family or for individual members, especially if the children were educated in German schools and were happy there.

Epilogue:
Looking through the Wall

Introduction
If you stay in Germany even for a relatively short time you will soon realise that West Germany is not the whole but only part of a Germany that was divided after the war following currency reform in the Western Zone and the Communist takeover in the Eastern sector.

Military zones
Germany is still divided into zones, British, American and French military zones. The American lifestyle has had a tremendous impact on the German way of life in commerce, industry and the media. The unique social composition (structure) of the British and American armed forces (respectively) means that these forces have a different effect on their own zones.

The Iron Curtain
Even as a visitor you will find it difficult to remain oblivious to recent memories of the Iron Curtain that divided not only the country between West and East but also Berlin. At one time there were frequent reports of East Germans being shot trying to escape to the West. Mercifully this is now only a horror of the past, however it may be in some people's minds.

Border areas
The Federal and the *Länder* border programmes explain why you will find universities or government institutions in the most unlikely places, such as a university at Bayreuth or Bamberg, and an administrative academy at Hof.

All this is an attempt to populate the border districts. Unfortunately it does not succeed or if it does it is only for certain periods during the year, for example during term at universities. But it

Epilogue

is artificial; German students are home birds and if they do not come from the surrounding border area, will go home at every available opportunity. Universities in the border areas empty over weekends or during vacations unless students have to stay to prepare for exams or attend vacation courses.

Most young people try to leave the border area for the more populous districts in the centre, leaving their border zones to the old people and tourists. Upper Franconia, for example, is most picturesque and full of art treasures — castles, museums, churches, etc. The quality of life — omitting the social-cultural side — can be higher in some border areas than in the towns.

The only problem is that sometimes these areas suffer from air pollution wafted over from East Germany or Czechoslovakia where regulations are not so strict or simply where filters do not exist. Sometimes the air is so bad in a border town in West Germany that there is a smog alarm and children are advised to stay at home!

The Iron Curtain extended to a length of 1,378km (some 1,500 miles), cutting not only the country into two but also villages, farms and traditional trade routes between East and West. This not only caused considerable personal misery but dislocation to commerce and industry. A city like Coburg, now on the border, used to be a staging point between Nuremberg and Leipzig (now in the GDR). Other cities are in the same predicament (although the dramatic developments in East-West relations since November 1989 are likely to have far-reaching effects). Such border areas are therefore given special subsidies to make up for this, be it in the form of tax reductions or other concessions.

Germany is two countries

One can live in Germany for many years and forget the Wall, the barbed wire, the Iron Curtain between East and West. In time it sinks into one's consciousness that there are two Germanies, not just one.

The German Democratic Republic

Over (now through) the Wall (*die Mauer*) the other side of the Iron Curtain is another Germany, with the same people, speaking the same language (with different dialects), eating the same

Epilogue

type, though not necessarily the same quality or quantities, of food. The East Germans are the same yet not the same. As yet there are still differences between East and West; shortages versus abundance; full employment versus a high rate of unemployment; a State-run economy versus a mixed one; in a word, all the differences which flow from this last essential difference, and which it will take time to change.

My experience has been — and I have been twice to the GDR on research — is that the East Germans, whilst they may have very few wordly goods compared to their fellow countrymen in the West — are, apart from some officials (and then very few), exceedingly friendly and kind to foreign visitors. They have virtually nothing and give everything. I remember my car, an English sports car, refusing to start on a Saturday morning in winter and in no time the local garage owner turned up at the hostel where I was staying and towed me along treacherously icy roads to his garage. He then spent the whole morning cleaning the carburettor which was choked with the local low octane petrol, altering the timing and then he charged me a very modest 24 *OstMark*. When I said how grateful I was, not only that he had done the job so well but had charged so little, he said: 'It's not money I'm short of, but time.'

That would never have happened in the Federal Republic where I suffered misery at the very poor and exceedingly expensive service. I am no communist and told anyone who cared to ask that I was an ardent monarchist, but – with the notable exception of when I recently applied to do further research and was rather curtly refused permission – I have always met with extreme kindness in the *GDR*. And there is no reason, especially now, why any English-speaking visitor, apart from those whose country has no diplomatic representation in the *GDR*, should be treated any differently. You do require a visa, which may usually be obtained on your behalf by a tourist agent. However, this may have changed by the time you read this book.

For the tourist the country, a third the size of the Federal Republic, is all the more beautiful now that old buildings are being restored — even statues of Frederick the Great and other historical figures are being replaced on their pedestals. Wander, or rather drive, in the footsteps of Goethe, Schiller, Bach, Haydn or Handel; visit the ancient cities of Weimar, Dresden,

Epilogue

Leipzig and East Berlin (capital of the GDR), the museums, art galleries and other places of cultural interest. Keep a sense of historical perspective and visit the sites of former concentration camps, Buchenwald and Ravensbruck; and don't omit the castle of Cecilienhof where Stalin, Roosevelt and Churchill signed the Potsdam Agreement in 1945.

You should not forget that you are in a communist country, that there are restrictions about taking photographs, changing currency illegally (the official rate is 1DM to 1 *OstMark*, although the true rate is approximately 1 to 5 or 6).

Few, if any would consider moving to East Germany, though many would like to visit the country as a tourist. It seems a pity not to do so because it may increase your sense of awareness about Germany itself and, of course, make you appreciate all the more the advantages of living in the West.

It could also make you consider the people who live the other side of the Iron Curtain and hope that one day that inhuman wall will come down with an assurance of peace.

Acknowledgements

Professor Dr Arthur Kreuzer (Professor of Criminology), University of Gießen.

Dr Dennis de Loof, University of Bamberg.

Herr Attaché Rainer Wilke (Consulate General of the Federal Republic of Germany, Osaka-Kōbe in Kōbe).

Herr Jürgen Abel (Press Officer), University of Bayreuth.

Fräulein Ursula Küfner (Secretary to the Press Officer), University of Bayreuth.

Frau E. Kieltsch (Tourist Officer), Bayreuth.

Herr Willie Tirstiege (Press Officer, Federal Bureau of Investigation), Herr T. Brecht (Federal Bureau of Investigation), Wiesbaden.

Herr Dipl.-Volksw. Wolfgang Berlinghof (Government of Oberfranken), Bayreuth.

Frau Anja Wiese (Tourist Office Berlin, Press Office 2), Berlin.

Herr Bernd Aßmann (Hypobank), Bayreuth.

Herr Stephan Lindner, Nürnberg.

Herr Gefried Hartel (Hamburg Münchener Health Insurance Company), Bayreuth.

Herr Karl Fürbringer (Public Employment Agency), Bayreuth.

Herr Oberregierungsrat Manfred Hartl, University of Bayreuth.

Herr Geschäftsführer Dr Lothar Zakrzewski (Student Welfare Organisation of Oberfranken), Bayreuth.

Frau H. Vater and Herr M. Röder (Federal Central Register), Bonn.

Herr Redakteur Gero von Billerbeck, Bayreuth.

Bestattung Himml Funeral Office, Bayreuth.

Acknowledgements

In conclusion I should like to thank Frau M. Lenich who typed part of the manuscript and Fräulein R. Strüder who painstakingly typed most of it with such dedication and devotion. There are a number of kind people who answered questions but whose names I either did not record in a rush or whose names I would have grievously misspelled had I attempted to do so. I am of course responsible for the mistakes which I have tried to reduce to a minimum, but one never can tell.

John A. S. Abecasis-Phillips

Bibliography

Facts About Germany. The Federal Republic of Germany (Bertlesmann Lexikothek Verlag, lastest edition) which can usually be obtained free from the Federal Office of Information: Presse- und Informationsamt der Bundesregierung (D-5300 Bonn 1), Welckerstraße 11, Postfach 2160, West Germany. This book is a mine of information and includes cultural matters.

These Strange German Ways (published by The Atlantic-Brücke e.V., Heschredder 52, D-2000 Hamburg 63, Federal Republic of Germany). This book is given free to members of the American Forces and so could possibly be obtained free from others who write in, though it would be only courteous to enclose something towards packing and postage. My copy weighs aproximately 180g.

The Federal Republic of Germany: A Country Study (Area Handbook Series). Editor Richard F. Nyrop (Department of The Army, Washington DC, 1982), obtainable from: Superintendent of Documents, US Government Printing Office, Washington DC, 20402. (Approximately US$15.) This is very good on German institutions.

Apart from books, I have found articles in English and American newspapers most instructive on Germany. Putting complicated German matters and events into English somehow makes them more comprehensible than they otherwise appear in German. Ditto unslanted television coverage.

Finally may I refer the reader to my own *Coping with Germany* (Basil Blackwell, Oxford 1989) which is intended for the short-term, as opposed to the long-stay visitor.

Index

accountants: use of, 22, 24
administration: importance of, 123
adult education, 37
advice bureau: for foreign students, 131
alcoholism, 160–1
alimony, 107, 108
American: influence, 87, 153, 192
AOK, Allgemeine Ortskrankenkasse, 29, 32
appearance: personal, 82
art galleries, 167

banks, 62–4; account slips, 63, 64, 65; charges, 65–6
Beamter, the official, 120, 122
border areas, 192–3
British: attitude to, 87
building societies: savings, 67–8
bureaucracy, 7, 120–6
BVA, Bundesversicherungsanstalt, 28, 188

cars, 41–3, 45; buying, 43, 66; insurance, 129; repairs, 58; theft, 55; using your own, 42
cheating, 79; at exams, 136–7
children, 106–8
chronic illness, 33
cinemas, 177
class system: lack of, 74, 91
cleanliness, 81–2
coffee, 172; and cakes, 177–8
contracts, 53–4
cooking, 167
crime rate, 185
cultural: life, 6; shock, 7
culture, German, 6, 7, 163–72; fringe, 166
customs: Duty, 55; and post office, 116–17; regulations, 50

dates: and German language, 112
death: and funerals, 189–90
demography, 162
dental treatment, 30
dismissal: from employment, 34
divorce, 107–8
documents: for residence permits, 132, 183; for university matriculation, 132
Double Taxation Agreement, 19–20, 21–2; Anglo-German, 22
drafts: money, 64
dress, 80–1, 82
driving: insurance, 44–5, licence, 44; psychology of, 45
drug addiction, 160, 161

education, 7–8, 35–40, 91, 147; adult, 37; German views on, 38; system, 36–7
eating out, 173–4
egalitarianism, 76–7
employment, 12, 190–1; agencies, international, 15; prospects, 15–16; situation, in Germany, 14
entertaining, 175–6
environment, 41, 150, 193
Ersatzkasse, Supplementary Health Scheme, 29, 32, 187
etiquette: official, 122–3
Eurocheques, 65
European Community, 155
examinations, 136–7
expenses: living, 235–6; and tax, 24

Federal government, 148
food, 168–72, 178; availability of British, 167–8; fattening, 178
foreign: exchange, of money, 64–5; status, 84

198

Index

foreigners: attitude to, 10, 87; voting rights, 150
furniture, 54–6

garages, 58; for repairs, 58
garbage collection, 60–1
gardening, 179
gardens, 82
German: citizenship, 184; Democratic Republic, 9, 192, 194–5
Germans, 85; scholarship of, 138–40
Germany, West: economy, 69–70; foreign relations, 153–6; politics, 8, 147–50; understanding, 84–5
Goethe, Johann Wolfgang von (1749–1832), 164–5
government: employees, 24–5; postings, 9–10, 45; by State, 130; Supplementary Insurance Scheme, 28
grants: student, 133–4
Green party, 151–2

health, 31, 160–1; insurance, 29–31, 32–3, 186–8
hierarchy: of German society, 74
Hitler, Adolf, 152
history: effect of, 5–9, 73, 84–5
housing, 50–3; buying, 66–9
housework, 56, 59
Humboldt, Wilhelm von (1766–1835), 144–5
humour: German, 85–6

identity cards, 121, 127
inflation, 62, 69
immigrant workers, 10, 88
import duty, 117
insurance: driving, 44–5; household effects, 49, 57; student, 134–5
integration: problems of, 72–3
interview techniques, 16
Iron Curtain, 192, 193, 195

jobs, 13–14, 15; *see also* employment

Krankenkasse, health insurance, 19, 187
Kultur: *see* culture, German

labour: cheap, 160
Länder, 73, 149, 154
language, 6, 10, 51, 74, 89, 105; business, 78; and culture, 111; and education, 35, 39, 147; north/south variations, 109–10; official, 110–11
landscape: German, 51–2
language, 6, 10, 51, 74, 78, 89, 105, 109–10, 111; and education, 35, 39, 147
laundries, 56–7
law, the, 127–30; study of, 145
laws, 9, 150
legal insurance cover, 128
life, 78; assurance, 27; span, 187–8
literature, 111, 165–6
living: expenses, 135–6; standard, 6, 13–14, 69; and workstyle, 13–14
Lokal, bar, 173
LVA, *Landesversicherungsanstalt*, 28, 188

manners, 89–91
marriage, 105–6; and tax, 106
military zones, 192
milk, 171
money, 17–25, 65, 67; German attitude to, 62
moonlighting, 78–9
Munich, 52, 181–2
museums, 167

national: insurance, 26–7; service, 155
noise regulations, 60
nuclear power: problems, 161–2, 165
number plates: car, 45

offences: fines for, 46
official act, *Verwaltungsakt*, 123–5
officialdom, 74, 120, 153
oil district heating, 61
old age, 188–9; pension, 185–6
orderliness, 56–7
Ortszuschlag, local allowance, 19

parents' council, 39–40
parking, 53
pastries and cakes, 171

199

Index

pay: equal, 95, 96
pensions, 8, 27–8, 185–6, 188
pets, 179–80
philosophy, German, 164
police, 45–6
politics, 8, 148, 149, 152
post, 58, 114–17
professors: university, 140–2
public holidays, 157

qualifications: need for, 12, 14–15, 96

rabies, 179
radio, 176–7
rail: cards, 47; travel, 47–8
refugees, 88, 150–1
regionalism, 73, 81; *see also* Länder
regulations, 120, 127
religion, 51, 85; State, 156–7
removals, 49–50
repairs, 58
renting accommodation, 52, 53–4
residence permit, 132–3, 183
retirement, 185–9, 190
returning home, 190–1

salaries, 17–19
Scheine, health certificates, 29–30
schools, 35–6, 37
security, 57–8; need for, 55
self-employed insurance, 27
seriousness, of Germans, 92–3
shopping, 168
skills: for employment, 14–15
smoking, 77
social: attitudes, 91–2; insurance, 27; life, 92–3
society: W. German, 72, 87–9
sport, 178–9
Sprechstunde, consultation hour, 122–3
staying on, 183–91; right to, 184
strikes, 157–8
students, 16, 78–9; protest, 142–6, 152; tips for, 131–46
Swiftair: postal service, 117
'system', the, 72

tax, 19–25; and house building, 69; and marriage, 106
taxcard, *Steuerkarte*, 19

teachers: and tax, 23
telephones, 60: use of, 117–19
television, 176–7
terrorism, 154–5
theatre: mobile, 167
tipping, 174–5
titles: professional, 93–4
tourism, 6, 180–2
towns: life in, 52
trade: schools, 37; unions, 129
traffic signs, 46–7
translation: work of, 137–8
transport, 41–8
trust, 80, 91
truth: attitude to, 79

UK tax: on overseas earnings, 20–1
unemployment, 14, 38, 88, 186; assistance, 34; benefit, 33–4; of graduates, 39, 40, 140, 145
unions, 13, 17; role of, 157–8
university: matriculation, 131–2; overcrowding, 145–6; staff, 140–2; students, 9, 38, 134; *see also* professors; students

valuables: sending by post, 115–16
VAT, German, 55–6, 117
Verwaltungsakt, official act, 123–5
videos, 177

water, 171–2
wealth tax, 25
weekend work, 159
will: need to make one, 25
wine, 172
Wirtshaus, pub, 173
women: pensions, 186; in politics, 148; role of, 94–5; status of, 90, 95–6, 105
work, 83; ethic, German, 13, 33, 76; style, 14
works council, 34, 76–7
written word: importance of, 86–7, 121

zip code (postal), 115
ZVS, *Zentralvergabestelle*, university admissions, 131

200